CW00821047

DETAIL Practice

Plaster, Render, Paint and Coatings

Details
Products
Case studies

Alexander Reichel
Anette Hochberg
Christine Köpke

Edition Detail

Authors:
Alexander Reichel, architect, visiting professor,
Lehrstuhl für Entwerfen und Raumgestaltung
(Chair of Design and Interior Design),
Technische Universität Darmstadt
Anette Hochberg, architect
Christine Köpke, architect

In collaboration with: Lisa Barucco

Drawings:
Sabine Nowak, Andrea Saiko

Editors:
Nicola Kollmann, Andrea Wiegelmann

Translators:
Translation Engineering GmbH, Munich

© 2004 Institut für internationale
Architektur-Dokumentation GmbH & Co. KG,
Munich
An Edition DETAIL book

ISBN-10: 3-7643-7110-2
ISBN-13: 978-3-7643-7110-4

Printed on acid-free paper made from cellulose
bleached without the use of chlorine.

This work is subject to copyright. All rights are
reserved, whether the whole or part of the
material is concerned, specifically the right of
translation, reprinting, re-use of illustrations,
recitation, broadcasting, reproduction on
microfilms or in other ways, and storage in
databases. For any kind of use, permission of
the copyright owner must be obtained.

Typesetting and production:
Peter Gensmantel, Andrea Linke,
Roswitha Siegler, Simone Soesters

Printed by:
Wesel-Kommunikation
Baden-Baden

This book is also available in a German
language edition (ISBN 3-920034-11-2).

A CIP catalogue record for this book is avail–
able from the Library of Congress, Washington
D.C., USA

Bibliographic information published by
Die Deutsche Bibliothek
Die Deutsche Bibliothek lists this publication in
the Deutsche Nationalbibliographie; detailed
bibliographic data is available on the internet
at http://dnb.ddb.de

Institut für internationale
Architektur-Dokumentation GmbH & Co. KG
Sonnenstrasse 17, 80331 Munich, Germany
Tel.: +49 89 38 16 20-0
Fax: +49 89 39 86 70
Internet: www.detail.de

Distribution Partner:
Birkhäuser – Publishers for Architecture
P.O. Box 133, CH-4010 Basel, Switzerland
Tel.: +41 61 205 07 07
Fax: +41 61 205 07 92
email: sales@birkhauser.ch
http://www.birkhauser.ch

DETAIL Practice
Plaster, Render, Paint and Coatings

House A

Typical constellations and detailed solutions for both interior and exterior plasterwork will be introduced using two examples. These examples are not real buildings, but are used to show a wide range
of solutions for a generalised, "normal"
project. The main difference between the
two examples is the type of wall construction.

House A is a typical 30 to 40-year-old residential building that has been upgraded
and optimized, both in terms of structure
and with regard to energy efficiency by
applying a composite system of thermal
insulation on top of the old rendering.
Simultaneously, this model can represent
an example of a new building, for which
detail solutions can be developed analo-
gously.

The project described here is a free-
standing multi-storey residential building
with 24 cm thick brick walls. This construction, which was common practice at
the time the building was erected, does
not meet the current requirements of the
energy efficiency act.

The ceilings are made of reinforced concrete throughout. The dividing walls may
be of masonry or drywall construction.
Window openings in different formats, the
largest of which are balconies built as loggias, give structure to the facades. The
old flat roof is planted.

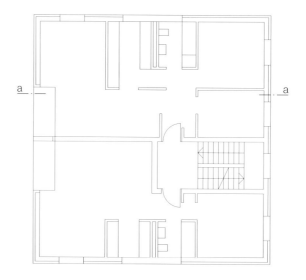

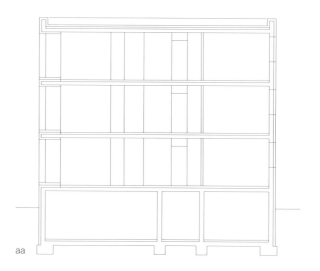

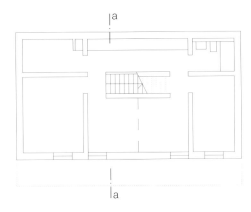

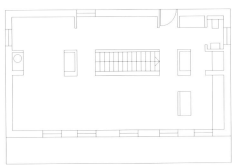

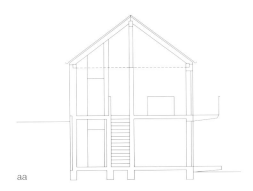

House B

House B is built from highly insulating bricks, 36.5 cm thick, covered in a 20 mm thick layer of lightweight plaster. This construction method allows for solid walls in keeping with current standards, achieving U-values of up to 0.30 W/m²K.

The building is comprised of two floors – an extended hillside level and a ground floor that extends all the way up to the roof. The load of the ridge roof, built as a purlin roof, is transferred directly to the walls. Bracing is provided by interior masonry walls and reinforced concrete ceilings. The windows are floor-to-ceiling, and can be fitted with a sunscreen, e.g. sliding shutters. The balconies are thermally separated from the main structure.

Even in the case of buildings to be renovated, simple construction details can be preserved provided the total energy balance of the building is taken into consideration. Rendering and plaster are employed in all their design variety.

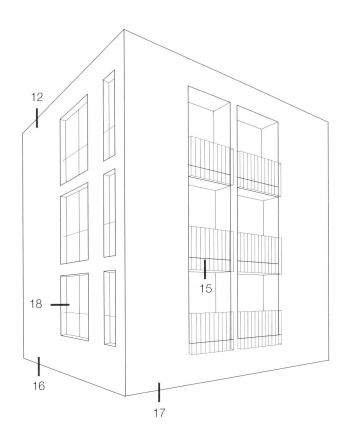

House A

12   Roof parapet
13   Window
14   Window
15   Balcony
16   Plinth, insulated cellar
17   Plinth, non-insulated cellar
18   Window panel, installation channel
19   Interior door

House A
Vertical cross-section
Roof parapet

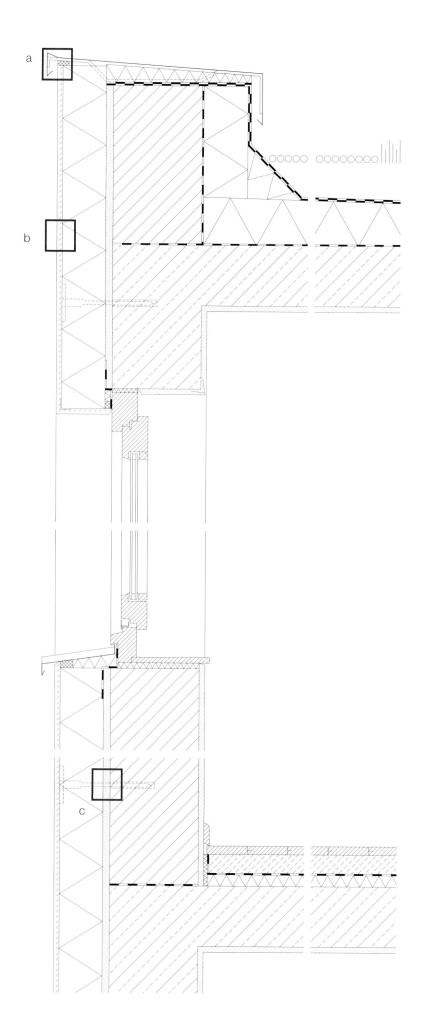

☐ a
The composite system of thermal insulation (ETICS system) is sealed to the fascia
plate with joint sealing tape to prevent
water from entering the insulation in driving rain. The system would fail if water
were to enter. The dimensions of the plate
are subject to the regulations of the roof-
ing trade.

Building height			at front a:
up to	8.0 m	≥	5.0 cm
up to	20.0 m	≥	8.0 cm
over	20.0 m	≥	10.0 cm

The projection, b, to the wall must be at
least 3.0 cm.

☐ b
CTI systems are multi-layer systems
approved by the building authorities. An
insulating material, usually rigid foam
sheeting or mineral wool is fixed to the
substrate with adhesive. The insulation is
completely covered with a reinforcing
material. A plastic webbing is smoothed
into the surface of it to prevent cracks
forming in the rendered surface. At corners which are particularly susceptible,
e. g. windows or jambs, diagonal reinforcement is incorporated into the surface
to increase the stability.

☐ c
The old rendering must be examined for
cracks and stability. Any particularly uneven surfaces must be levelled. Wall plugs
are required for additional anchoring of
CTI systems in the following cases: when
a soft insulation material is used and
when the building is greater than 8.0 m in
height, or where the substrate is in poor
condition with differences in the evenness
of more than 3.0 cm.
Every manufacturer has his own additional regulations linked to the building
authorities' approval.

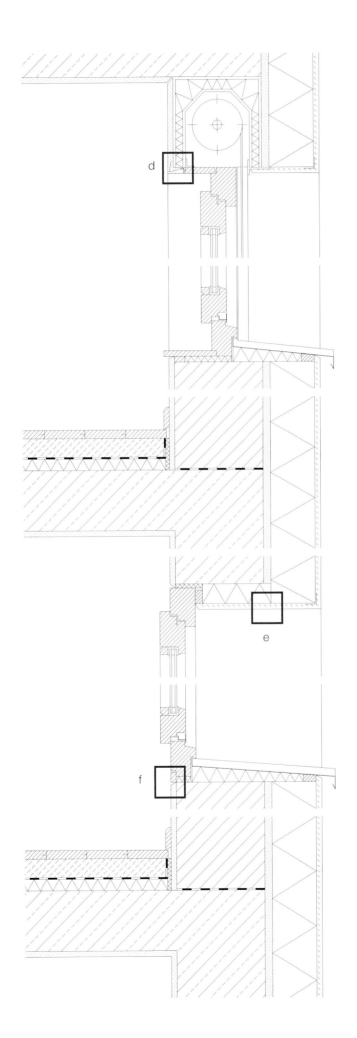

☐ d
If rolling shutter housings are present, the diameter of the rolled-up shutter determines the position of the window. The housings are pre-assembled and supplied already insulated. They are rendered after installation. A maintenance opening must be left, which separates a rail from the rendering.

☐ e
The position of the window in the wall determines the appearance of the building. Simultaneously, it also has consequences for the construction, since insulation must always be flush with the window to ensure optimised building physics. During renovation works, the windows are often replaced and additional insulation added to the building. The most straightforward solution is to fit the window at the outside edge of the wall so that the composite insulation system can be laid without any recesses. If the windows are positioned closer to the interior surface of the wall, the insulation must also be laid around the edges of the opening.

☐ f
A high degree of precision is required during construction so that the window frame and the interior plaster are flush. This requires appropriate attention during the planning phase. The different materials expand at different rates when the temperature changes, and must therefore be separated from one another. This can be achieved using a dummy joint in the plaster or by applying joint tape around the whole perimeter of the wooden frame. The use of the traditional trowel joint shown here is sufficient. It is achieved by running the trowel along the joint in the fresh rendering. In this way, a defined break-line is created between the two materials.

House A
Isometric drawing, horizontal cross-section
Window

☐ a
The window plate is set into a groove
below the weather bar and attached to
the parapet with adhesive. The edges of
the window plate are angled upwards
and cut into the composite insulating
system so that the water runs onto the
plate from the drip head and does not
penetrate the space between window
and rendering. The windowsill, like the
window frame, is completely edged with a
joint tape or a flush-mounting strip to separate it from the plaster. To prevent cracking, the stresses, which are caused by
the different expansion rates of the different materials when the temperature
changes, must not be transferred to the
rendering. This would make it easier for
water to enter and cause damage to the
construction.

☐ b
The window joint must be rain and wind-
proof. To achieve this, the space between
the wall and the window frame is filled
with insulating material. Depending on the
joint permeability required, the joint is
either sealed using joint tape and then
rendered, or an additional seal material is
used. This additional seal is usually either
a self-adhesive construction film or neo-
prene tape. Wooden windows acc. to DIN
68121 and all window constructions with
a circumferential seal (groups A and B)
which are fitted in a house not taller than
20.0 m do not usually require an additional seal. The energy-efficiency regulations must still be followed, however,
meaning that a very water-tight building
shell may be required depending on the
works being undertaken. The position of
the window, e. g. at the front of the
facade, also requires additional measures
to be taken against wind and rain.

☐ c
The window frame is fixed in position
using iron ties or special window frame
ties which can be bolted directly through
the frame and into the wall. This results in
a gap of around 2 cm between wall and
window frame depending on the building
tolerance. The plaster in the gap is
matched accordingly to give an even wall
surface.

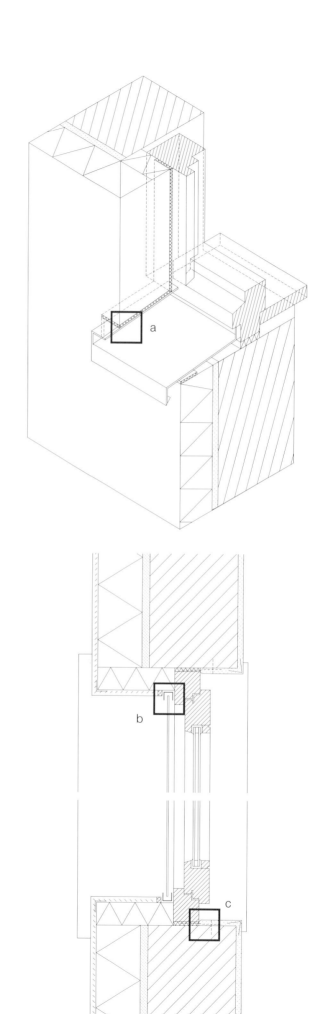

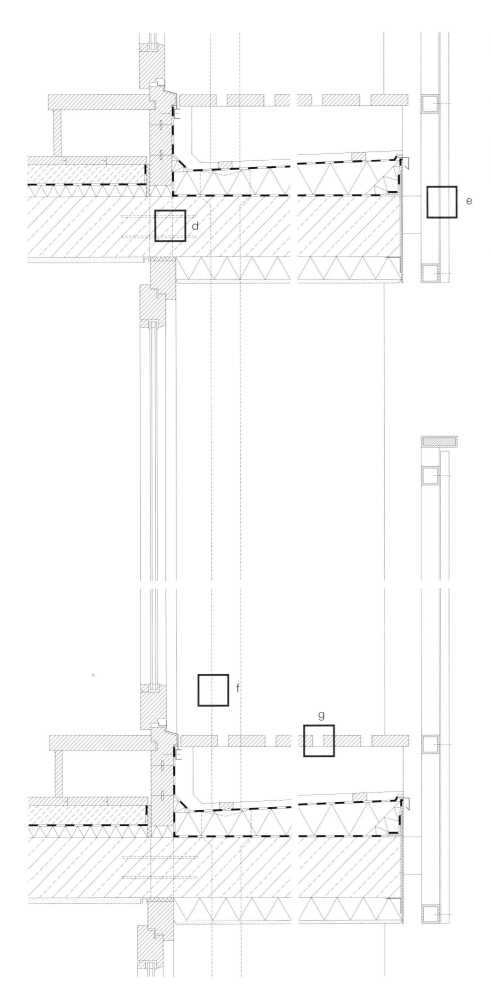

□ d
The balcony base slabs are particularly susceptible to stresses caused by changes in temperature and are good thermal conductors. For this reason they are generally insulated from the building itself using a thermally insulated connector – trade name Isokorb – reinforced for tensile and compressive loading. Since this technique was unknown when older buildings were erected, the concrete slab must be insulated at least on its upper and lower surfaces when renovating. As a rule of thumb, 10.0 cm insulation thickness corresponds to 1.0 m thickness of concrete. For a balcony base slab this means that the concrete slab must be covered in insulation over a distance of at least 1.0 m. The front does not then require insulation and can serve as a mounting surface for the balcony fastening.

□ e
In order to provide as homogeneous a front view as possible in this example, the railing with timber battens is continued along the entire height of the balcony structure, made up of the thickness of the insulating layer plus the upstand.

□ f
Balconies and loggias require floor drains. With closed parapets, a 40 mm minimum diameter emergency drain must be provided in addition to the floor drain. With open railings, rainwater can be drained off into the drainpipe from the roof. Rainwater may only be drained through water-shedding moulding if this does not adversely affect any third parties. In renovation projects, core drilling can be used to retrofit direct drains with a flange and ring screen. The centre of the pipe is located some 20 cm from the wall, since the seal is achieved using a gasket seal whose adhesive width is predefined depending on the drain diameter.

□ g
A timber floor grid in sections, which can be lifted for cleaning and allows water to run off, makes a simple covering for balcony floors. The surface lies 15 cm above the upper edge of the water-bearing layer of the balcony's sealing layer. The substructure lies on a protective mat, which prevents the sealing layer from being damaged. The wooden step – also usable as a bench – acts as a transition to the interior.

House A
Vertical cross-section
Plinth, insulated cellar

☐ a
The plinth area starts at the surface of the
ground and is least 30 cm high. Compression-proof rigid foam sheets are
used since the plinth must be splash-
proof and it has a high mechanical loading. Some manufacturers supply special
plinth protection sheets which can be laid
in the insulation above the plinth. These
can be used to protect areas subject to
increased knocks, e. g. walls against
which bicycles are often rested, or soft
insulation in lower areas.

☐ b
After the top layer of rendering or coating
has dried through, suitable damp-proof-
ing, e. g. an insulating cement-based
slurry, is applied to areas in contact with
the earth and must join with the sealing
layer of the building. This protects the
rendering from rising damp. To protect
the rendering from damage during filling,
and as a run-off layer, a napped plastic
sheet is used to cover it.

☐ c
The insulation used below the surface of
the ground is also compression-proof
rigid foam sheeting. Since this insulation
must be effective even when it takes up
water, it is known as perimeter insulation.
The insulation is attached to the sealing
layer course using a bituminous or
cementitious compound. The substrate
must first be damp-proofed in accordance with DIN 18195 to a height of 30 cm
above the ground surface.

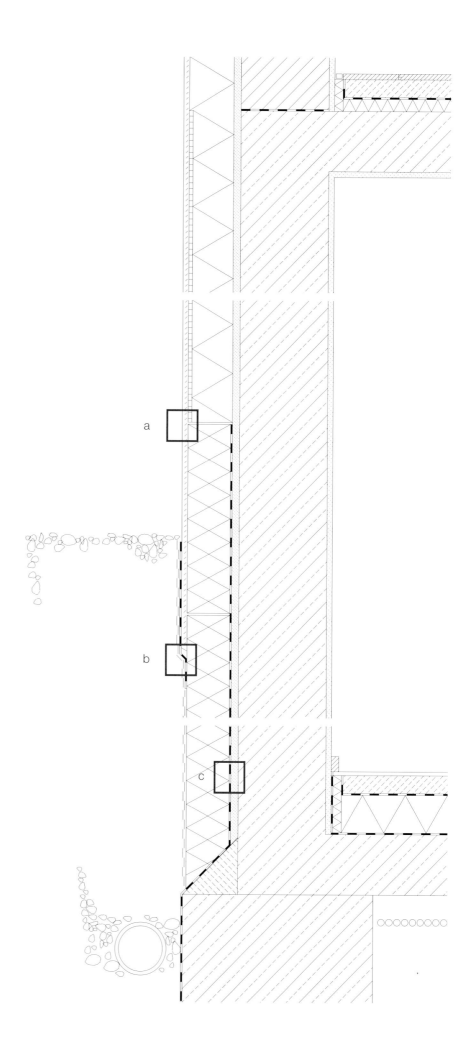

House A
Vertical cross-section
Plinth, non-insulated

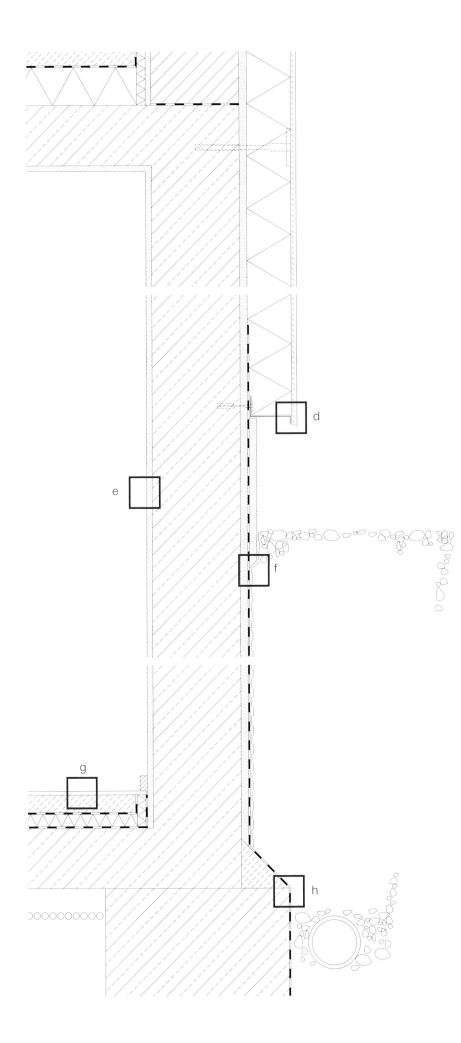

☐ d

For uninsulated cellars the insulation must extend only 50–80 cm beyond the "warm space" – the insulated part of the building. Below this level, a sealing layer and plinth rendering are sufficient. The resulting offset is constructed creatively as a plinth edge. Depending on the rendering surface, a drip head may have to be embedded in the upper layer of the coating.

☐ e

The interior rendering in uninsulated rooms must be more resistant to moisture than in heated areas. Lime plaster, or lime-cement plaster should be used in cellars, garages or wet rooms for this reason. Gypsum plasters can only be used under certain conditions due to their hygroscopic properties.

☐ f

To protect the sealing layer, a drainage sheet is placed in front of the wall. A napped plastic sheet is usually suitable, however corrugated plastic or porous insulating material can also be used. The sealing layer must be protected from sharp filling material and drainage must be possible without any standing water.

☐ g

The floor screed can be protected with a 2-component floor coating instead of a sensitive floor covering. The layer of aqueous epoxy resin or acrylate is 1–2 mm thick. It is applied with a roller or rubber trowel in two or three stages. Since rising damp often causes a high osmotic pressure in the floor slab, the coating which is used should allow diffusion to prevent later blisters from forming.

☐ h

The transition from foundation to wall must be concave to ensure that water can drain underneath the floor slab or to the drainage pipe. There must be at least 20.0 cm between the pipe and the upper edge of the rough concrete of the cellar floor. According to DIN 4095 it must be laid in a bed of 8/16 grade gravel. The remaining excavated material is compacted in layers and back-filled.

House A
Horizontal cross-section
Window panel, installation channel

☐ a
Due to the distance between the insulation and the ground, suitable sub-con-
structions must be provided for the load-
bearing connections since the insulation
cannot carry loads. A further possibility is
to transfer the load directly to the walls via
extensions. Since the rails for the floor-to-
ceiling windows are usually fitted after
rendering to prevent contamination of the
metal and avoid extensive patching
works, brackets are to be provided. To
this end, metal angle brackets are
attached to the wall using plugs. It must
be ensured that a sufficient gap is left for
fastening, and that the wall material can
carry the load. The subconstruction is
rendered in one operation. The railing
frame including the filling is pre-fabri-
cated in the workshop and need only be
screwed together on site. It should be
noted that welding on site not only makes
protection against rust more difficult, but
may also melt the rigid foam insulation.
Slotted holes allow for tolerances. To prevent even the low thermal conduction of
the metal angle brackets and ensure the
rendered surface is flush, almost all manufacturers offer integrated mounting elements, e. g. compression-proof insulating
blocks for heavy loading and spiral plugs
for light loads such as lamps or letter
boxes.

The facade cannot usually be insulated
and rendered without the need for scaffolding. When erecting scaffolding it must
be ensured that sufficient space is left
between the wall and the scaffold to fit
the insulation or railing.

☐ b
The joint between a gypsum plasterboard
plumbing wall and a wooden panel is
subjected to a large amount of movement
during construction. For this reason, the
corners of the individual plasterboard
sheets are covered by a separator strip of
oil packing paper. This can be plastered
over and is still capable of absorbing dif-
fering variations. The metal studs are separated from the substrate by a soft joint
sealer or a mineral wool separator strip.

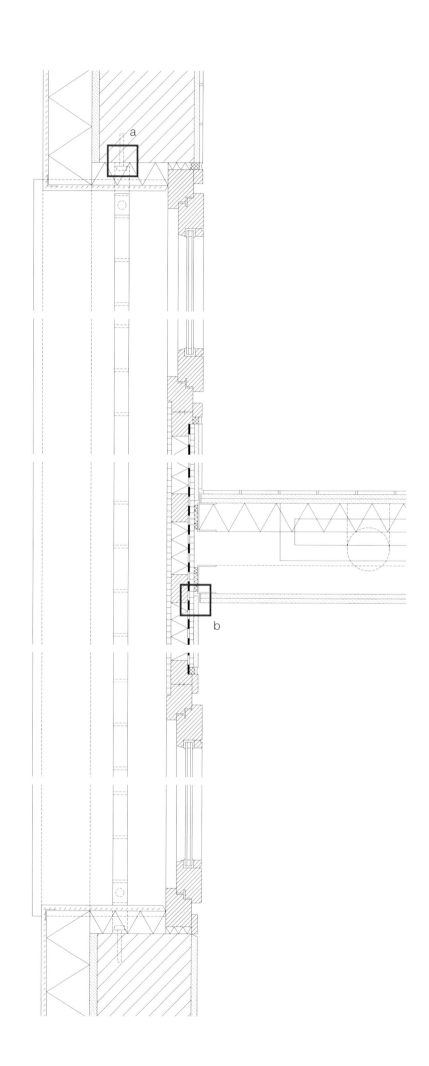

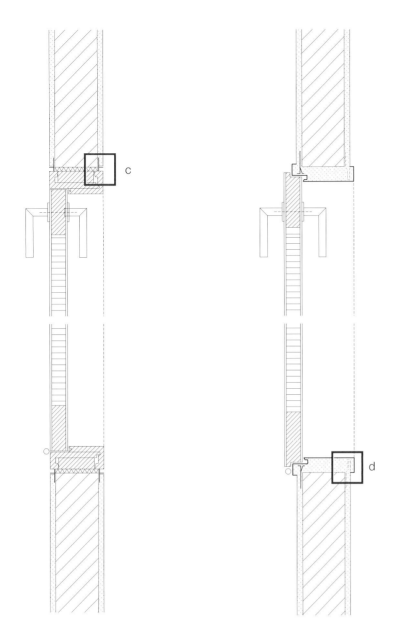

☐ c

The upper and vertical jamb surfaces of the opening in the building shell are often joined to the doorframes. The doorframes can be made from solid wood or wooden materials. The wooden door case is the most solid option amongst the otherwise boarded type jamb frames. For interior doors with a butted leaf and no additional joggle, this means that the leaf and wall are flush. Fitting a plank as a bedding dot in the jamb ensures that the thickness of the wall jamb is the same at all points. A simple wooden batten or metal strip can also be used as a plasterer's derby, preventing an overly large gap between the wooden frame and an uneven rendering surface. The jamb itself need not be rendered. To achieve a clean edge where the rendering meets the opening, galvanised steel dummy joint sections are attached to the seam between the wall and the wooden frame. Skirting boards, which may stand off from the wall surface, may have to be decoratively joined to the door frame. The frames are usually delivered pre-primed and receive the final coat of paint on site once most of the building work is completed.

☐ d

One of the most commonly used frames is the industrially manufactured steel enclosure frame. Here, hot-rolled or cold-drawn steel sheet, 1.5–3.0 mm thick is shaped to a profile in such away that it encompasses the wall. Simultaneously, notches are formed to take the seal. The inner dimension of the frame, the so-called rim width, relates to the wall thickness including rendering. Enclosure frames are usually fitted into the jamb before rendering. They can be fixed in position using welded masonry ties, plug or nail anchors, which are attached to the un-rendered edges of the jamb. The gaps around the frame are filled with plaster. For fire doors, regulations demand a ventilated cavity and the use of a larger number of anchors. The steel casing is supplied pre-primed with an anti-rust primer and is then painted on site.

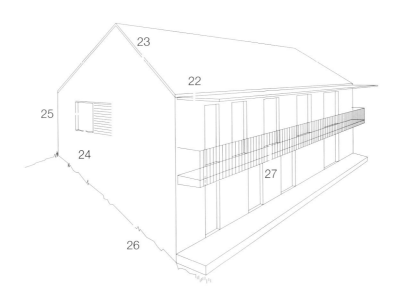

House B

22   Roof, eaves
23   Roof, gable board
24   Window, sliding shutters
25   Window, sliding shutters
26   Plinth, insulated cellar
27   Balcony

House B
Vertical cross-section, elevation
Roof, eaves

☐ a

The transition from wall to roof covering
requires careful planning. Particular care
must be taken with the foot which affects
the pediment elevation. The construction
of the gable board and eaves varies
depending on the roof construction –
ventilated or not ventilated – and the roof
material – metal or tiles. Small and cut
tiles are used on the joint with the gable
board and the upwardly inclined pediment elevation. An edged perforated
plate forms the upper joint to the eaves,
serving as an edge trim and clean edge
to the rendering, and as a ventilation
grille and insect screen for the roof construction.

☐ b

The inferior purlin of the roof framework
lies on top of the wall and is clad with
smaller tiles. This ensures thermal insulation and an even rendering base.

☐ c

Before rendering, the brickwork must be
checked for its suitability to act as a
rendering base. It should be flat jointed
in accordance with DIN 1053 and the
guidelines on offsets should be adhered
to. Defects, open mortar pockets and any
hollow fronts on toothed bricks must be
filled with masonry mortar. If the rendering – e. g. over joints – is concave, it will
not adhere well and the rendering will
crack in this area. For this reason, the
brickwork should be flat jointed. If dry
butt joints are used, joints wider than
5 mm should be closed on both outer surfaces using a suitable masonry mortar.
Weatherproof rendering can then be
applied in a layer with an average thickness of 20 mm.

☐ d

The grain size of the exterior render used,
which is also responsible for the textured
finish, should not be too small. Small,
structurally harmless hair cracks are more
noticeable in smooth-faced plaster than in
coarser plaster. A grain size of 1–4 mm is
usual for exterior rendering.

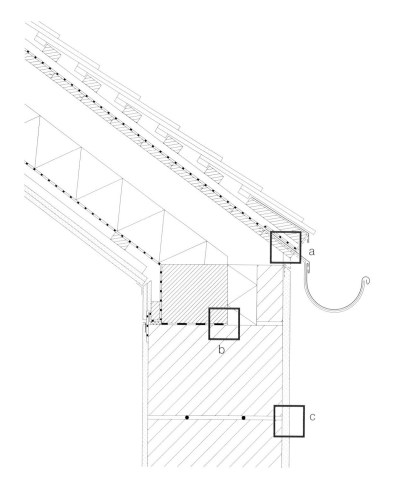

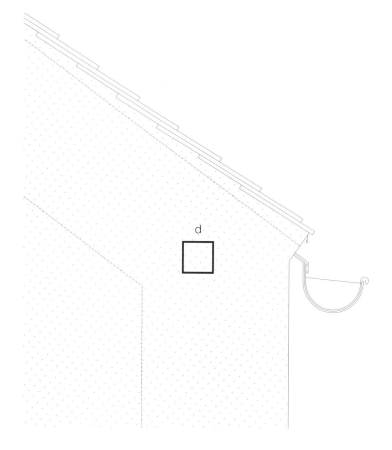

House B
Vertical cross-section
Roof, gable board

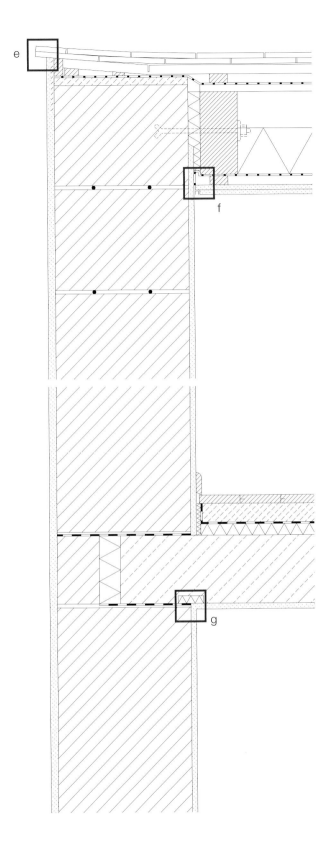

☐ e

A very simple type of roof edging is flush-plastering. This is achieved by plastering, with no division, up to and under the roof tiles. Meshing, e. g. galvanised wire or plastic mesh, must be laid into the under-coat plaster as a base to prevent the plaster from cracking in this area. The meshing covers the different materials over their whole area and carries the tensile stresses. The outer roof tiles protrude at least 3 cm, storm clips are never used as additional securing.

☐ f

The vapour barrier continues to the masonry wall. Affixing the sheet to the rafter with a roof batten ensures a continuous and therefore impervious joint. The break-through points are carefully lined. However, care must be taken to shape the last piece of sheet into a loop. This loop carries the material-dependent stresses. The protruding sheet can either be plastered over or stuck to the plastered wall with double-sided sticky tape, whichever the construction schedule allows.

☐ g

Building elements may deform due to:
• thermal processes caused by, e. g., sun or shade;
• hygric processes caused by, e. g., water or steam;
• material-chemical processes.
Brickwork and concrete behave differently under these circumstances. Above all, the shrinking and creeping of concrete can lead to stresses in the bearing area – e. g. due to the shrinkage of a concrete ceiling under load. To combat this, the concrete ceiling and the brickwork supports must be moveable. Bitumen board under and on top of the bearing area of the concrete ceiling and an inserted screed insulating strip reduce indirect stresses. In addition, the lower sheet prevents the concrete from entering the core holes of the bricks and creating an acoustic bridge. The front edge of the concrete ceiling slab is additionally insulated because of its high heat transmission, and finished off with a half-brick to form a uniform base for rendering.

House B
Vertical cross-section
Window, sliding shutters

☐ a

The brick lintels are prefabricated elements made from a brick shell filled with reinforced concrete. They are standard building elements available in various standardised widths and lengths and form the tension boom of the finished lintel. The bearing depth must be at least 11.5 cm. The elemental length of the lintel is between 1.0 and 3.0 m.

☐ b

A wooden, metal or light metal sliding shutter can be used in place of a roller shutter as protection from the sun and against break-ins. Each shutter may weigh up to 80 kg, is approx. 40 mm thick and runs in rails at the top and the bottom. All mechanical parts are concealed so that rain, snow or dirt cannot directly affect the rails.

☐ c

The rails for the sliding shutters are fixed to the wall with screws using corrosion-resistant masonry dowels before rendering. To avoid cracking due to different material stresses in the rendering, the anchor plate must be covered by meshing – a thin rigid foam sheet would be even better – as a base for the rendering. The rendering joins the steel rail with a seam or trowel joint.

As an alternative to this elegant but complex transition, the rail can be laid directly onto the rendering at the end of the construction work, as shown in this example. The gap between wall and rail must be carefully sealed to prevent water from entering. To prevent plaster from breaking away due to excessive contact pressure, a thermally insulating spacer is placed between the rail and the wall.

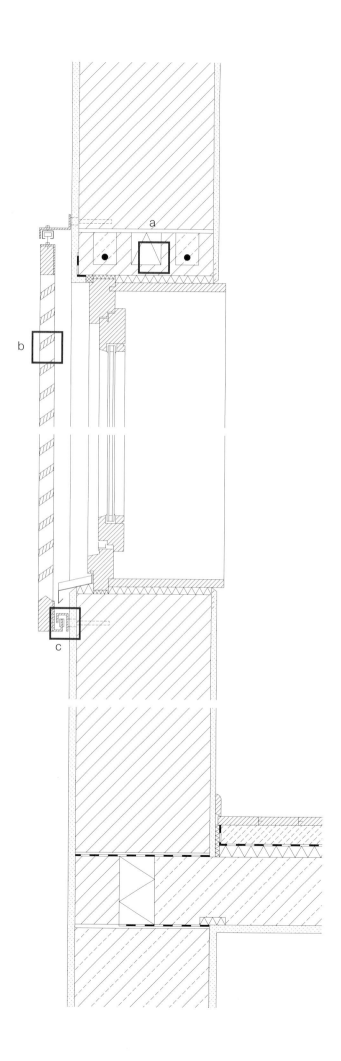

House B
Horizontal cross-section
Window, sliding shutters

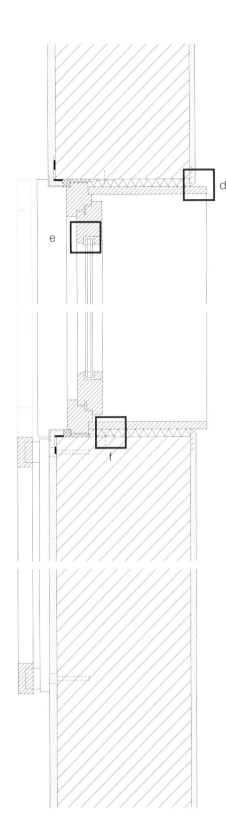

☐ d

The rendering adjoins the wooden board with a trowel joint. It is sensible to allow the edge of the windowsill to protrude by about 3 cm, since it is laborious to align the jamb boards flush with the rendering and apply this accurately. To enable the edge to be rendered, the window itself lies approx. 2 cm behind the outer unfinished edge.

☐ e

Exterior wooden parts must be dimensionally stable. Windows, for example, are required to have a scumbling protective coating to protect against blueing, fungal attack and distortion. The windows are generally painted with coloured paint or with a glazed finish at the works and installed pre-painted. The window frames must therefore be protected from the caustic effects of plaster falling on them during any rendering works following their installation. The protective measures required should be separately detailed in the invitation to tender.

☐ f

The windows are anchored in the brickwork at 80 cm intervals using metal brackets known as clamp irons or window screws. Where the window construction is not rabbetted, the joint must be well sealed. According to the currently valid energy-saving regulations of 2002, joints must be sealed against wind and driving rain from the exterior and be vapour-proof on the interior. Since there is a large temperature gradient in the gap between the interior and the exterior, condensate is to be expected the closer the window is placed to the exterior. It is therefore even more sensible to insulate the jamb in single-shell constructions. The insulation can be clad with a circumferential wooden frame, which doubles as a windowsill and joins the different materials.

House B
Vertical cross-section
Plinth, insulated cellar

□ a
To compensate for the difference in heat transmission through the concrete and bricks, the concrete cellar wall is given additional insulation. A reinforced and therefore thin concrete wall enables the use of perimeter insulation without recesses in the outer facade. The rigid foam sheeting is fixed to the sealing layer using a bituminous adhesive.

□ b
Exterior plinth rendering must be sufficiently strong, i.e. generally having a compressive strength of 10 N/mm^2. It may be only slightly hygroscopic and must be resistant to damp and frost. Generally, a cement rendering is used to render the plinth up to the surface of the ground and it is applied on a layer of galvanised mesh sprayed with rendering. The thickness of the rendering can be greater than 20 mm, since this area in particular is in need of protection. The sealing layer below the plinth rendering must include a bonding course in the form of an insulating cement-based slurry.

□ c
A brick or concrete cellar wall must be protected from ground damp and pressurised water. In general this is achieved using a thick two-component bituminous waterproofing system. Before the actual coating is applied, an undercoat is applied and a scratch coat may be applied as a levelling course. The dry coating should be 5 mm thick for ground damp and 6 mm thick for rising water. The coating is continued over the concave moulding on the exterior of the foundation.

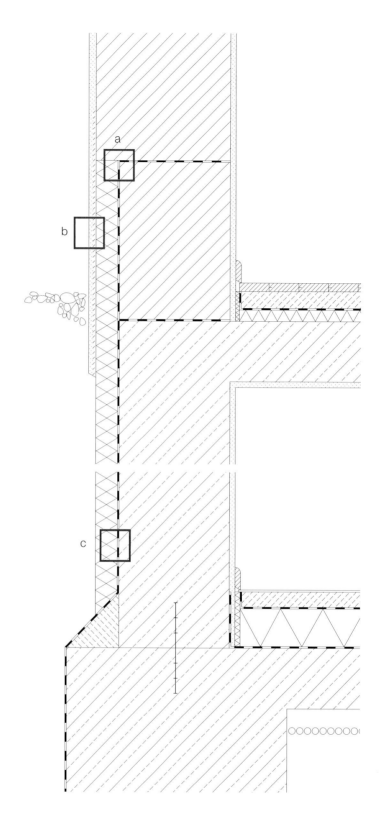

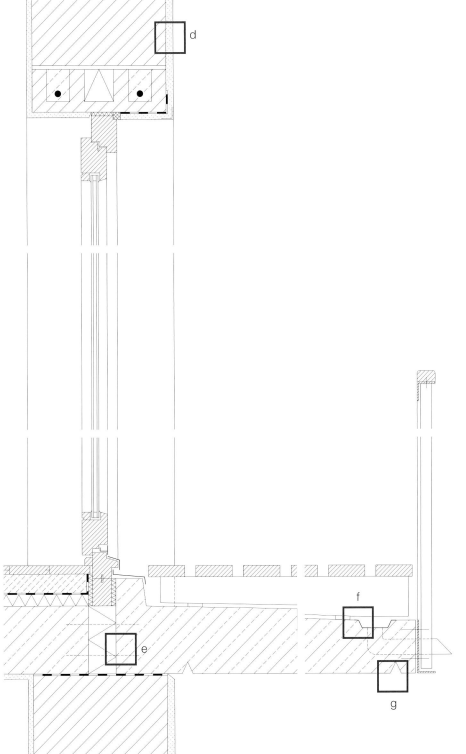

d
Rendered facades on the weather face of the building are exposed to moisture. The rendering must be water-repellent, but also allow water vapour to permeate from the interior to the exterior. This is also true of the paint on the facade, whose properties must be selected to be appropriate for the substrate. The relationships of the permeability of water, water vapour and carbon dioxide to each other must be modified accordingly, so that paint and rendering function together as a unit.

e
The balcony is made from a pre-cast concrete unit which is fixed to the intermediate floor via an Isokorb.
Isokorbs are standardised prefabricated elements made up of reinforcement cages and rigid foam insulating blocks, which are positioned between the floor and the balcony as a thermal barrier. The elements have a maximum length of 1.0 m and are available in floor thicknesses of 16–25 cm. Depending on their construction, the Isokorbs are built and cast into the formwork or are already fastened to the prefabricated element.

f
To prevent water from running off haphazardly, excess water is collected in a gutter at the end of the slab and channelled into a rainspout where it is drained directly.

g
To prevent dirt marks caused by run-off water, protruding elements are fitted with a drip head which breaks up the water film.

Plaster/Rendering

Rendering and plasterwork shape the character and appearance of a building.

The rendering or plaster acts as a protective skin and takes on a number of diverse functions. The rendering or plaster system is determined by the choice of building materials during the planning phase. Walls, rendering, plaster and possible paints or coatings must be chosen to suit each other, so that they work together correctly as a system.

Rendering and plasterwork are applied during the last phase of the construction process and are therefore often carried out at a time when the budget has already been exhausted. Imprudent use of components, which are not suitable for use with the rest of the system, can lead to permanent damage of building elements.

Durable systems must be well-planned, implemented at the appropriate time, and correctly maintained. For this reason, it used to be common practice to whitewash houses regularly. Regional building traditions are a mine of expert knowledge and mastery which ought to be reactivated, particularly in light of the Europeanisation of the construction process, to promote a widening diversity of designs. Architects, craftsmen and manufacturers are called on to take on this challenge at an early stage.

1   Nizwa, Oman, traditional opening construction

Mortar is defined as a mixture of binders, aggregates (particles) and mixing water. Mortar is divided into two groups – rendering and plastering mortar and masonry mortar – each defined by their use. Mortar is further defined by:

- its state: fresh mortar (ready-to-use) or hardened mortar,
- the place of manufacture: site-made mortar (mixed on site) or factory-made mortar (mixed in the factory and delivered ready-to-use).

Plastering/rendering
Plastering/rendering, as defined in the standard, is a single- or multi-layer coating of plastering or rendering mortar applied to walls or ceilings with a defined thickness (other coatings as a top coat are also possible). Its final properties develop only after hardening.

The major component by volume is the aggregates. The mortar also contains binders, in smaller quantities, which "glue" everything together and are responsible for the hardening process and hardening type, as well as much smaller quantities of admixtures with special properties.

The usual ratio of 3:1, sand to lime, in the lower layers has remained the same in most recipes since antiquity. In some recipes this ratio is maintained until the last daub. Other recipes recommend the use of more lime (i.e. finer, softer, less sandy mortars) in the final layers, along the lines of the old painters' rule: fat on lean. Mortars which contain smaller amounts of binder are weaker and sand more readily. Those which contain larger amounts of binder shrink considerably, which can cause shrinkage cracks, (gypsum plasters are an exception: they swell and are volumetrically stable).
The average thickness of standard mortars should be 20 mm (min. 15 mm) on the exterior and 15 mm (min. 10 mm) on the interior. Which mortar, technique and plastering/rendering system are chosen depends on the surface to be treated, the expected loading and the desired surface finish.

In old buildings, the moisture content of the various materials has come to an equilibrium, which may be disturbed by desiccative measures and hydrophobic coatings, causing shrinkage or the efflorescence of salts.

Technical properties of plastering/rendering mortar
- The Young's modulus of the mortar should be smaller than that of the surface to be treated.
- The water absorption coefficient should be 0.5 kg/m²h^{0,5} (water-retarding).
- The adhesive strength test should generate a crack in the plaster/rendering base, or the adhesive strength must be greater than $\beta hz \geq 0.1$ N/mm^2.
- The compressive strength âd of the mortar should be less than that of the base. The determining factors in the strength achieved are the type of binder used and the ratio of binder to aggregate (B/A).

Exterior rendering has the task of levelling the brickwork, closing up small gaps (windproofing) and forming a protective coating to protect the building from the weather. It serves to protect and decorate the facade.

Table 2
Composition of the most important exterior renders according to their type/binder and their structural properties.
[1] A limited addition of cement is allowed.
[2] Domestic kitchens and bathrooms are not counted as wet rooms.
[3] For exterior plinth rendering on brickwork with a strength class of 6, P III mortars may, as an exception, have a minimum compressive strength of 5 N/m^2. They must meet the demands of water-repellent plastering/rendering systems.

w-value:
water absorption coefficient

μ-value:
water vapour diffusion resistance coefficient

s$_d$-value:
diffusion-equivalent air layer thickness

	Mortar groups	Type of mortar	Type of binder	Aggregate
mineral mortars	P I a	non-hydraulic lime mortar	non-hydraulic lime putty or hydraulic lime	sand
	P I b	hydraulic lime mortar	hydraulic lime putty	sand
	P I c	mortar with hydraulic lime	hydraulic lime	sand
	P II a	mortar with eminently hydraulic lime and rendering and masonry binders	eminently hydraulic lime or rendering and masonry binders	sand
	P II b	lime-cement mortar	lime putty or hydraulic lime and cement	sand
	P III a	cement mortar with hydraulic lime addition	cement and hydraulic lime	sand
	P III b	cement mortar	cement	sand
	P IV a	gypsum mortar	anhydrous gypsum and plaster of Paris	–
	P IV b	sand gypsum mortar	anhydrous gypsum and plaster of Paris	sand
	P IV c	gypsum-lime mortar	lime putty or hydraulic lime and anhydrous gypsum or plaster of Paris	sand
	P IV d	lime-gypsum mortar	lime putty or hydraulic lime and anhydrous gypsum or plaster of Paris	sand
	P V a	anhydrite mortar	anhydrite binder	sand
	P V b	anhydrite lime mortar	anhydrite binder and lime putty or hydraulic lime	sand
	loam rendering according to DIN 18 350			
	can be combined with P I + P II	loam mortar	clay fraction	sand/gravel, cut straw
organic mortars, (coatings)	P Org. 1 (synthetic resin plaster)	alkali-resistant coating material	polymer resin	organic and mineral possible
	P Org. 2	coating material		

Most standards, both German national and European standards (DIN and EN), quoted here are intended for new buildings.

The new European standard
DIN EN 998-1: 2003-09
Specification for Mortar for Masonry, Part 1, replaces the sections in DIN 18550-1 to -4 which deal with the manufacturing of factory-made plastering or rendering mortar. DIN EN 998-1: 2003-09 replaces the plastering mortar groups P I a, b, c, P II, P III, P IV a, b, c, d and P V in DIN 18550-1 with classifications according to compressive strength (CS I-CS IV), capillary water absorption (W 0, W 1, W 2) and thermal conductivity (T 1, T 2).

Interior hot — Exterior cold
External rendering
Water vapour — Water vapour resistant
Internal plastering — Moisture head
Water vapour permeability

External rendering
Water vapour — Permeable to water vapour

3

It introduces new abbreviations for the types of mortar according to their properties and/or field of use: GP: General purpose rendering/plastering mortar, LW: Lightweight rendering/plastering mortar, CR: Coloured rendering mortar, SC: Single coat rendering mortar for external use, R: Renovation rendering mortar, T: Thermal insulating rendering mortar, FP: Fracture pattern. In addition, it regulates the following:
· Addition of single coat rendering mortar for external use
· Specification of the reaction to fire according to the European classification
· Replacement of the third-party and self inspection processes for the attestation of conformity with a defined evaluation of conformity process 4 (manufacturer's statement) according to the Construction Product Directive.

The CE label of conformity consists of: the CE symbol, the name or identifying mark and registered address of the manufacturer, the last two digits of the year in which the marking was affixed, the number of the European standard, a description of the product and information on the regulated characteristics.

"The properties of rendering and plastering mortars depend essentially on the type or types of binders used and their respective proportions". (Quote from the introduction to DIN EN 998-1). DIN EN 998-1, however, no longer provides for a classification of plastering or rendering mortars according to the type of binder, and the details to be provided in the CE label do not include the binder. The properties required of the hardened mortars overlap greatly within the ranges given for the compressive strength in classes CS I to CS IV.
The requirements of EN 998-1 must therefore still be carefully coupled with the criteria used when selecting the plastering or rendering system.
The choice of a particular plaster or rendering system is determined by the choice of the binder, its stability and water vapour diffusibility. The decisive criterion for an invitation to tender is knowledge of the mortar recipe, the setting process and the compatibility or incompatibility of the binder and aggregates. Since the new standard does not require sufficient information in the manufacturer's labelling, it is advisable to obtain the necessary information directly from the manufacturer himself.

Aggregate[1]	Minimum compressive strength [N/mm²]	Mainly suited to	w-value [kg/m²h^0.5]	μ-value	s_d-value [m]
cement	no requirements	Interior and exterior plaster/rendering for low loads Exterior render, water-retardant, only with AM Exterior render, water-repellent, only with AM	> 2.0	20	s = 0.02 s_d = 0.4
cement	no requirements		> 2.0	20	
–	1.0	Interior plaster for general requirements including wet rooms[2] Exterior render, water-retardant, only with AM Exterior render, water-retardant, only with AM	> 2.0 where AM < 0.5	20–30	s = 0.02 s_d = 0.4–0.6
–	2.5	interior plaster with higher abrasion resistance including wet rooms Exterior render, water-repellent, only with AM	< 2.0	20–30	s = 0.02 s_d = 0.4–0.6
–	2.5	exterior render with higher strength	> 0.5 with ZM < 0.5	15–35	
–	10[2]	cellar wall exterior rendering Exterior plinth rendering[3]	0.5	50	s = 0.02 s_d = 1.0
–	10[2]				
White lime	2.0	Interior plaster, corresponds to machine-applied plaster of Paris, bond plaster and ready-mix plaster acc. to DIN 1168 part 1.	machine-applied plaster: 5.0–15	(8) 10	s_d = 0.25
White lime	2.0	interior plaster	Bond plaster	ca. 18	s_d = 0.25
–	2.0	Interior plaster	Ready-mix plaster: 5.0–15	5–6 5.0–15	
–	no requirements	Interior plaster	5.0–15	5–6	
–	2.0	Interior plaster, natural gypsum with additions of argillaceous limestone, marl or iron oxide and therefore not pure white in colour			
–	2.0	Interior plaster			
	dried: 2–3 Light adhesive: 0.1–1	Interior plaster, can be used on the exterior, with great limitations	10–20	5–10	s = 0.02 s_d = 0.10–0.2
–		Interior and exterior plaster on a load-bearing, strong, mineral and polymer-coated surface, water-repellent	0.1	100	s = 0.005 s_d = 0.5
		Interior plaster			50/200

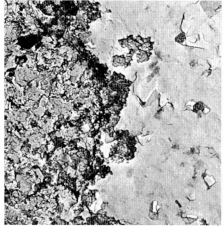

4

5

6

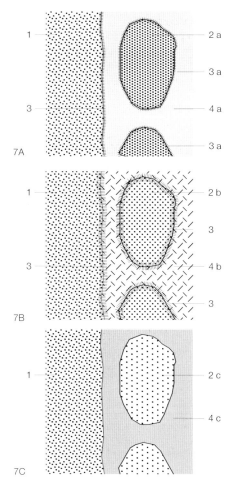

7A

7B

7C

Mineral binders are divided into the following groups: lime binder, calcium silicate binders, calcium aluminate binders, calcium sulphate binders and silicate binders. Table 2 shows how the various binders fit into these groups. The group to which the mineral binder belongs determines the type of hardening. The two hardening processes are hydration and carbonation.

The most important binders used for plaster today are hydraulic or eminently hydraulic limes and cements. The type of the binder determines the strength, the hardening time, the frost resistance, the salt resistance and the water resistance of the plaster. The compressive strength of the mortar increases in the following order (listed by binder type): non-hydraulic lime, hydrated hydraulic lime, hydraulic lime, eminently hydraulic lime and cement. Hydraulically hardening limes form the transition from non-hydraulic lime to cement. Calcium carbide and calcium silicate are formed during the hardening of hydraulic limes and non-hydraulic limes with hydraulic additions. Silicates are formed at the boundary between hydraulic lime and hydraulic additions.

Limes can be mixed with each other in any ratio. Non-hydraulic lime can be mixed as desired with cement or gypsum and anhydrite binders. Calcined gypsum or anhydrite binders cannot, however, be mixed with hydraulic binders, since sulphate expansion may occur.

Since non-hydraulic lime and cement binders can be mixed in any ratio, they can be used to make plasters with a variety of different properties, depending on the primary hardening process. Table 11 gives an overview of the binders, their relative fractions of carbonatic and hydraulic hardening, their hardening times, their classification according to the different mortar groups and their preparation and use.

4 Completely carbonated white-lime mortar; intergrown calcite crystals
5 White-lime mortar
    Left: fine hydrate crystals
    Right: laminar, intergrown calcite crystals (carbonated)
6 Lime-cement mortar, completely hardened, acicular calcium silicate hydrates of the cement between the calcite crystals
7A Lime plaster with latent hydraulic aggregate (P I A)
7B Eminently hydraulic lime plastering mortar (P II a)
7C Cement plaster (P III)
8 Plaster cycle
9 Lime cycle
10 Hydration, phases of the hardening of cement

Hardening processes of the binder (drawing 7A–7C):

1 brick plaster base
2a aggregate: trass sand, pozzoulana
2b aggregate: trass, fired clay
2c aggregate: quartz sand
3 silicate formation at the boundary
3a the formation of calcium silicates at the boundaries increases the strength
4a calcium carbonate, porous
4b calcium carbonate and silicate mixed crystals, porous, medium strength
4c hydrated cement, impervious, high compressive strength

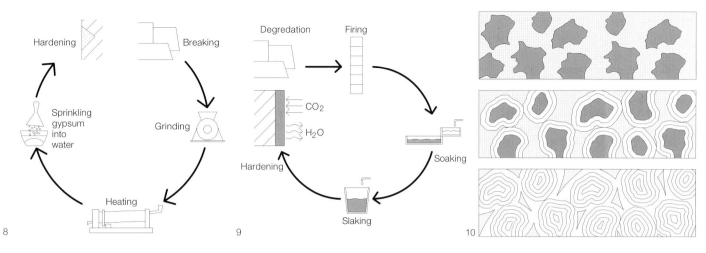

8   9   10

Hydration of plaster

Firing at low temperatures:

CaSO4 · 2H$_2$O + heat (below 300 °C) →
Calcium sulphate-dihydrate
CaSO$_4$ · 1/2H$_2$O + 1 1/2 H$_2$O
Calcium sulphate hemihydrate + water

Firing at high temperatures:

CaSO$_4$ · 2H$_2$O + heat (over 300 °C) →
Calcium sulphate-dihydrate
CaSO$_4$ + 2H$_2$O
calcium sulphate + water

Mixing:

CaSO$_4$ · 1/2H$_2$O + 1/2 H$_2$O →
Calcium sulphate hemihydrate + water
CaSO$_4$ · 2H$_2$O + heat
Calcium sulphate-dihydrate

Carbonation of lime

Ca(OH)$_2$ + H$_2$CO$_3$ → CaCO$_3$ + 2H$_2$O The
CO$_2$ in the air and the mixing water form
carbon dioxide (H$_2$CO$_3$), which reacts
with the calcium hydroxide to form calcium carbonate, which has only limited
water resistance.

Firing:

CaCO$_3$ + heat → CaO + CO$_2$
limestone + heat quicklime + carbon
dioxide

Slaking:

CaO + H$_2$O → Ca(OH)$_2$ + heat
quicklime + water slaked lime + heat

Hardening:

Ca(OH)$_2$ + CO$_2$ → CaCO$_3$ + H$_2$O
slaked lime + carbon dioxide →
limestone

Non-hydraulic limes harden slowly in air.

Hydration of cement

The starting material decomposes in this
reaction. The addition of water molecules
and the formation of OH- groups leads to
the formation of hydrates. Hardening will
also occur under water.

Portland cement

3CaO · SiO$_2$ + (3-x+y)H$_2$O →
xCaO · SiO$_2$ · yH$_2$O + (3-x)Ca(OH)$_2$
Water-resistant calcium silicate and calcium hydroxide are formed, which are
transformed into calcium carbonate using
CO$_2$.

Table 11
shows the various binders and their relative fractions
of carbonatic and hydraulic hardening.
The binders can be mixed with each other in any
ratio. This enables the production of plasters with very
specific properties.

Table 11, hardening of the binders

Hydration						Carbonatic binding							
CaSO$_4$· 1/2H$_2$O + heat + 1 1/2 H$_2$O = CaSO$_4$ · 2H$_2$O + heat						Ca(OH)$_2$ + CO$_2$ = CaCO$_3$ + H$_2$O				Hydraulic binding 2 (3 CaO · SiO$_2$) + 6 H$_2$O = 3 Ca · 2 SiO$_2$ · 3 H$_2$O + 3 Ca(OH)$_2$			
calcium sulphate hemihydrate + water + water = calcium sulphate dihydrate						hydraulic lime + carbon dioxide = limestone + water				tricalcium silicate + water = calcium silicate hydrate + hydraulic lime			
gypsum plaster	sand gypsum mortar	gypsum-lime mortar	lime-gypsum mortar	anhydride mortar	anhydride lime mortar	non-hydraulic lime	hydrated hydraulic lime	hydraulic lime	eminently hydraulic lime	plaster-mortar binder	lime cement	cement lime	cement
P IVa	P IV b	P IV c	P IV d	P V a	P V b	P I a	P I b	P I c	P II a	P II a	P II b	P III a	P III b
chemically neutral						carbonatic carbona	hydraulic to carbonatic	carbonatic to hydraulic					hydraulic
						slakeable	not yet slakeable	not slakeable					not slakeable
Hardening: 1–20 hours						months to years	months	approx. 28 days					approx. 28 days decades (carbo-nation)
engineering gypsums				natural gypsums plaster rock		pit lime	Roman cement trass lime Roman cement		trass cement				

Hydration = water is chemically bound
Carbonation = reaction caused by the CO$_2$ in the air = progressive, slow hardening over a period of years

12

13

14

Gypsum

Calcined gypsums harden in air. The raw material, plaster rock, is present in nature as a dihydrate (hydrous calcium sulphate) and as an anhydrite (anhydrous calcium sulphate). It is fired in a rotary kiln either at low temperatures, of up to 300°C, or at high temperatures of up to 1000°C. The water of crystallisation is completely or partially removed from the plaster rock in this process. Anhydrous gypsum is formed by firing at low temperatures, and plaster of Paris is formed by firing at high temperatures. If the powdered gypsum is mixed with water, the gypsum reacts exothermically with the water to form the raw material again, calcium sulphate dihydrate ($CaSO_4 \cdot 2H_2O$).

Lime

Quicklime ($CaCO_3$, calcium oxide) and carbon dioxide (CO_2) are formed when limestone ($CaCO_3$, calcium carbonate) is fired at temperatures below the sintering limit of 1250°C. The quicklime is slaked by adding water. The slaked lime (hydraulic lime, lime paste, calcium hydroxide) almost doubles its volume as it expands. Slaked lime ($Ca(OH)_2$) hardens back to limestone ($CaCO_3$) when mixing water (H_2O) is added, using CO_2 from the air. The water which is liberated evaporates.

Cement

Cements solidify and harden both in air and under water. They are hydraulic binders. Cements are made from limestone and clay, limestone being the major constituent. The hydraulic components – silicon dioxide (SiO_2), aluminium oxide (Al_2O_3) and iron oxide (Fe_2O_3) – are contained in the clay. The finely ground raw marl meal is fired in a rotary kiln at 800 –1450°C to form cement clinker. The cement clinker is ground to a fine cement with the addition of plaster rock or anhydrite as a retarder.

The hydration of the cement is due to a reaction between the cement particles and water. It begins as soon as water is added, generating heat. Gelation starts at the grain boundaries of the cement and ends with the complete transformation of the cement grain to hydrate.

The smaller the grains of cement, the more rapidly the cement gel transforms to solid hydrated cement. The hydration of larger grains can take years. Dehydration can interrupt the hydration process, the addition of water can reactivate it. The hardened product is water resistant.

Table 15   Classification of mineral binders into material groups

Material groups	Main phases of the binder	Classification of binders
Lime binders	Calcium oxide, CaO Calcium hydroxide, $Ca(OH)_2$	Quicklime Hydraulic lime Hydraulic carbide lime
Calcium silicate binder	Tricalcium silicate, $3\,CaO \cdot SiO_2$ (C_3S)[1] Dicalcium silicate, $2\,CaO \cdot SiO_2$ (C_2S)[1]	Portland cements Portland cements with interground materials
	Tricalcium aluminate, $3\,CaO \cdot Al_2O_3$ (C_3A)[1] Aluminate ferrite phase, $2\,CaO\,(Al_2O_3 \cdot Fe_2O_3)$ ($C_2(A, F)$)[1]	Cements with interground materials
Calcium aluminate binders	Monocalcium aluminate, $CaO \cdot Al_2O_3$ (CA)[1] Calcium dialuminate, $CaO \cdot 2Al_2O_3$ (CA_2)[1]	High-alumina cement Aluminous cement
Calcium sulphate binder	Calcium sulphate hemihydrate, $CaSO_4 \cdot 1/2\,H_2O$ Anhydrite, $CaSO_4$	Gypsum binder Anhydrite binder
Silicate binder	Potassium water glass, $K_2O \cdot nSiO_2 \cdot H_2O$	Potassium water glass Silicate of soda

[1] common abbreviation for clinker phases in silicate chemistry

The type of hardening of the mineral binders can be deduced from the material group to which they belong. The classification of the binders according to their material group is given in table 15.

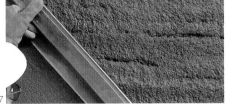

Plastering / rendering system

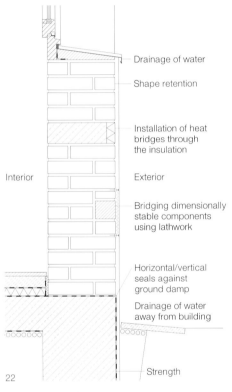

Drainage of water

Shape retention

Installation of heat bridges through the insulation

Interior   Exterior

Bridging dimensionally stable components using lathwork

Horizontal/vertical seals against ground damp

Drainage of water away from building

Strength

22

The layers of plasterwork or rendering, which, combined together and dependent on the base, fulfil the required characteristics of the plasterwork or rendering, are termed the plastering or rendering system. Even a single-coat rendering can be considered a rendering system. A coat or skin of plaster or rendering is defined as a layer of one type of mortar applied in one operation (in one or more throwing-on), which is not yet set. Following a period of one day per 1 mm plaster thickness, a second skin of the same thickness is applied. The drying time for overly thick layers of plaster must be taken into account during preparation of the construction schedule. There are single- and multi-layer plastering and rendering systems. The lower layer is known

as the undercoat or base coat, the upper layer as the finish coat or final rendering. The base coat levels any unevenness and absorbs any differences in stress between the surface being treated and the finish coat. It is coarser and rougher than the finish coat. The water vapour permeability of plasters and rendering should be as high as possible and should increase from the interior to the exterior.

Plastering / rendering rules

1 Ensure a mechanical bond between the plaster and the surface material (scratch out any seams, coarse machine-applied plaster);
2 Use only coarse aggregates for machine-applied plaster and base coat plaster;
3 Forceful throwing of machine-applied plaster and base coat mortar;
4 Check whether the surface requires pre-wetting (especially for lime mortar in the summer months);
5 Ensure the strengths of the plaster and surface are compatible. The plaster should not be stronger than the surface, otherwise the plaster and not the surface will carry the load.

Most of the movement, which a building experiences, occurs in the first few months after completion of the shell. Allowing an adequate waiting period before commencing the plastering / rendering will reduce the risk of structural damage. It can take up to two years for brickwork with a high level of residual moisture to dry out completely. The risk of cracks appearing in the plaster/rendering due to shrinkage is very high. If exterior rendering is carried out before the interior plasterwork and the laying of screed floors, this can be detrimental for the quality of the plasterwork (cracking), especially during the winter months. If the wall is uneven such that there are

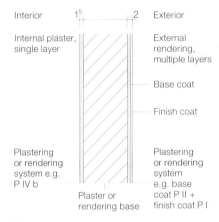

Interior   1.5   2   Exterior

Internal plaster,   External
single layer   rendering,
                                  multiple layers

                                  Base coat

                                  Finish coat

Plastering   Plastering
or rendering   or rendering
system e.g.   system
P IV b   e.g. base
                                  coat P II +
           Plaster or   finish coat P I
           rendering base

23

differences of more than 5 mm in the thickness of the plaster layer, then two layers of plaster must be used. The differences in thickness would otherwise cause stresses in the plaster system leading to cracking.

16 Undercoat plaster is applied
17 The undercoat plaster is levelled using a darby
18 The undercoat plaster is combed
19 The finish coat is applied
20 The finish coat is levelled with a toothed darby
21 Depending on the type of finish coat, the surface is textured or scratched with appropriate tools
22 Requirements of the plaster base
23 Plaster system
24 Individual skins of plaster, getting finer from the bottom to the top layer.

24

25 26 27

Aggregates

By volume, these make up the largest proportion of the mixed plaster and together with the binder therefore influence the quality-defining properties of the plaster such as density, porosity, compressive strength and weather and frost resistance. Aggregates are classified according to their structure and purpose:

• dense structure: sand, crushed sand, gravel, granular materials
• porous structure: pumice, tuff, expanded clay, crushed brick
• hydraulic: trass, pozzoulana and santorin earth
• coloured: black basalt, schist, coloured quartz sand, porphyry, green syenite
• glittering: mica, crushed shells, cullet
• workable by a stonemason: shell limestone, sandstone, limestone and tuffstone granulate.

Specific textured finishes can be obtained by careful selection of the type and composition of sands. The way in which the plaster is applied (by hand or machine) has an influence on the recipe, particularly the use of coarse grades and admixtures. Coarse grades cannot be applied using a machine, but can easily be applied by hand. A mixture of different sizes of sand reduces the size of the interstices (spaces between the individual grains). The amount of binder required for the particular aggregate mixture depends on the mixture of sand sizes and the shape of the grains – long, elongated or compact. Compact grains have the best shape, and result in dense packing. The coarsest grade has the greatest influence on the texture of the plaster.

The evenness of the plaster's colour is determined by the finer grades and the colour of the binder. Historic plasters generally contain aggregates that occur locally. This is often what makes them unique.

Admixture

Admixtures are partly manufacturer-specific: each manufacturer has his own recipes and patents. They are added to influence the properties of plastering mortars, e.g. their water-repelling capability, porosity, adhesion with the surface, elasticity and setting time. Admixtures are usually organic materials (see table "admixtures for plastering mortar", appendix, p.101).

Additives

Additives are finely distributed additions. They influence the properties of the mortar and, unlike admixtures, their volume must be taken to account. Additions may only be used if they do not have a negative effect on the mortar. They must not change the strength and stability of the mortar or the setting and hardening of the binder, or may only change these as expressly intended.

Fillers

These are rock and ceramic meals for thin-laminated plasters.

Fibres/reinforcing materials

These materials improve bending and tensile strength and reduce the susceptibility to cracking. Animal hairs, straw, reed, shredded bast, wool and plant fibres were used as reinforcing materials in historic plasters.

Mixing water

Water from the public mains is suitable.

Aggregates and pigments

Aggregates and pigments increase the decorative potential of the materials. The surface of the facade obtains a depth and clarity intrinsic to the material. This variety is best observed in historical plasterwork.

There are many different styles of plastering and rendering – even today there is a large variety of hand-crafted styles in addition to the standardised, crack-resistant, easy-to-maintain, and guaranteed impervious, but somewhat lacklustre ready-mix plaster.

Mortar pigments

According to DIN 53 237, only light-fast, lime-fast and cement-fast pigments may be used for coloured plasters and rendering. Pigments may only be added in quantities which do not affect the ability of the mortar to bind (up to 5% of the quantity of dry binder). The more dry powder pigment is added, the dryer the mix will become. Strong colours which require a large quantity of pigment are therefore something of a problem. As an alternative, plaster coloured with organic or mineral pigments is used as a finish coat, or a coloured paint is used.

There are organic pigments, which are usually chemically manufactured, and inorganic pigments, which are normally of mineral origin.

The following are considered to be natural pigments, e. g.:
- Earth pigments, cleaned, dried, finely ground ores (yellow ochre, iron oxide, sienna etc.),
- Mineral pigments made by heating sulphur, clay, soda (ultramarine blue, vine black etc.),
- Spinel pigments, volcanic minerals (spinel yellow, spinel orange, spinel blue etc.).

A wide range of colours can be achieved using coloured plaster alone. All plastering mortars can be coloured. Historic plasterwork can be a source of inspiration. Lime plaster with ground charcoal, for example, is a beautiful shade of grey. If the correct binder, responsible for the weather resistance of plasters, is chosen, then no paint is necessary. Coloured mineral and silicate plasters may, however, dry to a cloudy finish. This is not a technical defect and is therefore not a valid ground for complaint. To reduce discussions about guarantees, however, many manufacturers and craftsmen recommend an equalising coat.

Any paint or coating must be chosen to suit the plaster system in use. The wrong paint could ruin the whole plaster system. If, for example, lime plaster is coated with a sealing paint, then CO_2 cannot be exchanged with the air and water cannot transported to the exterior. Both of these processes are essential for the gradual hardening – over a period of years – of lime plaster, which has the ability to heal itself when fine cracks form during hardening. The sealing coating chokes the plaster, which means that the plaster sands off beneath the coating, losing its strength. In extreme cases, more water is taken up when it rains than can dry out again through the coating. For a lime plaster with a high capillarity, this means that it becomes soaked through and, figuratively speaking, "drowns". According to DIN standards, plasters and renders generally have a lifetime of 50 years. This plaster, however, would be ruined within a very short period of time.

The colour shade of the plaster should not be neglected. Even lighter shades have a higher surface temperature than plain white due to diffuse radiation, allowing the plaster to dry more quickly after rain. This prevents, among other things, algal growth.

25 Different types, sizes and textures of aggregates
26 Fillers
27 Mica flake additives
28 Coloured pigments
29 Pigment mill

30

DIN 4108 (11) lists three classes of exterior rendering for protection against rain and moisture. These are defined by the amount of rainfall and the strength of the wind.
Group I: no special requirements
Group II: water-resistant
Group III: water-repellent.

Classification is with reference to the rainfall map. The selection of a suitable rendering/coating system with the required protection against rain must be based on the regional conditions, the annual rainfall and the height of the building. According to Helmut Künzel, the rain protection properties of a wall are evaluated from its change from wet to dry and vice versa. The figures derived from these processes are 1) the water absorption coefficient (w) of the plaster, which gives us information about the water absorption when the wall is subjected to rain, and 2) the diffusion-equivalent air layer thickness (s_d) which describes the drying process.

The capillary structure (absorbency of the rendering) is not only defined by the type of binder, aggregates and mixing and the hardening during application, but most importantly by the afterhardening processes. The same applies for the strength of the rendering. Keeping rendering with carbonatic and hydraulically hardening binders moist, for example, promotes hardening. If the mixing water enters the surface material too quickly, the rendering will dry out or fire on, resulting in poor strength. In carbonatic hardening, the bonding of CO_2 from the air together with H_2O is responsible for the afterhardening over a period of years.

The requirements for water-repellent renders, which were specified in the Plastering and Rendering Standard DIN 18550 part 1, published in 1985, are formulated by Künzel primarily on the basis of tests carried out with synthetic resin plasters. This DIN specification defines the properties required of water-repellent exterior rendering. According to Künzel, the numbers given are based on the following principals: the smaller the w-value, the greater the s_d-value can be, so that moisture absorbed during rainfall can be given off by diffusion; if the rendering is more absorbent (higher w-value), a smaller s_d-value is therefore required.

An important prerequisite for the evaluation of the protection against rain is the determination of w and s_d on the same surface sample. The maximum w- and s_d-values are limited so that excessive water uptake or excessively long drying periods are avoided. According to DIN 18550, the following is valid for water-repellent exterior rendering:

$w \cdot s_d \leq 0.2$ kg/(mh$^{0.5}$)
$w \leq 0.5$ kg/(m^{2}h$^{0.5}$)
$s_d \leq 2.0$ m

Rendering with no special requirements
Rendering belonging to rain protection group I is classed as absorbent if it has a water absorption coefficient w > 2.0 kg/(m^{2}h$^{0.5}$).
The rendering is neither water-resistant nor water-repellent

Table 31
Comparison of the capillary water absorption according to the old DIN 18550 standard and the new EN 998-1 standard

DIN 18550	EN 998-1[1]
Water-resistant rendering system $w \leq 2.0$ kg/m^{2}h$^{0.5}$	W 1 c ≤ 0.4 kg/m^2 min$^{0.5}$
Water-repellent rendering system $w \leq 0.5$ kg/m^{2}h$^{0.5}$	W 2 c ≤ 0.2 kg/m^2 min$^{0.5}$

[1] The previous standard unit of measurement m^{2}h$^{0.5}$ has been changed to m^2 min$^{0.5}$.

Table 32
Classification of the rendering types according to requirements, composition, use and water absorption

Mode of action requirement group	Composition	Use/properties	Water absorption coefficient w-value
Rendering with no special requirements Non water-resistant rendering	Lime cement rendering Lime rendering Gypsum rendering Loam rendering Silicate rendering	Sound-absorbing rendering Levelling plasters Fire-proof rendering Compartment mortar Compression renders Sacrificial rendering Porous base rendering Shielding rendering	> 2.0 kg/m^{2}h$^{0.5}$
Water-resistant rendering	Lime cement rendering	Reinforcing rendering Lightweight rendering Renovation rendering Crack bridging plasters Thermally insulating rendering	2.0 kg/m^{2}h$^{0.5}$
Water-repellent/ capillary water-impervious rendering	Cement-lime rendering Silicone resin rendering Cement rendering (P III b)	Renovation rendering Coloured rendering	0.5 kg/m^{2}h$^{0.5}$
Rising water resistant rendering	Cement rendering, specially tested	Sealing rendering Plinth rendering	no absorption of water Load scheme: Rising water

Lime plaster / rendering

The term "lime plaster" or "lime rendering" is not exactly defined. Until the development of the cement industry in the 19th century, multi-layer lime rendering systems were usual. The "classic" lime mortar plasters are white lime plasters made with the quicklime (white hydrated lime) from lime pits.

Mason's lime is the most important mineral binder for plastering and rendering mortars. Lime plasters are used as base and finish coats, as interior plasters and exterior rendering. They can be used on any absorbent, mineral surface.

An important factor in the manufacture of the binders is the relationship between the initial composition of the raw ingredients and their firing temperatures. Mason's lime is made by firing limestone ($CaCO_3$) at a temperature below 1250°C. The quicklime (CaO) which forms then reacts with water to form slaked lime, hydraulic lime, $Ca(OH)_2$. In the dry slaking process, enough water is added to form a dry hydraulic lime powder. In the wet slaking process, water is added in excess. A hydraulic lime-water putty is formed, which can be stored as pit lime for longer periods of time. Plaster or rendering made with pit lime is more flexible.

Lime mortars which have only hydraulic lime binders harden via carbonation. Carbon dioxide (CO_2) from the air combines with the mixing water to form carbonic acid (H_2CO_3), which reacts with the slaked lime to form limestone with limited water resistance. The water evaporates. The lime cycle can also occur in the opposite direction.

Using moisture and CO_2 from the air, lime plaster can combat the effects of weathering due to thermal deformation and

frost cracking, as well as crystallising and hydrogenating salts. For this reason it is often the weather side of an older building with historic plasterwork, which is best preserved.

A sufficient supply of CO_2 must be ensured for interior plasterwork so that carbonation can occur. The high humidity of the air in interior spaces must be taken into account. The addition of puzzolanic additives can increase the strength of non-hydraulic limes. The Romans took advantage of this effect in their cement-like material opus caementicium.

If the hydraulic fraction of lime plaster is increased, the strength becomes increasingly similar to that of lime-cement plasters. Hydraulic lime made by firing lime marl (limestone containing clay) at 1200°C, lies somewhere between non-hydraulic lime and cement. Both relatively soft non-hydraulic lime mortars, which harden only via carbonation, and much stronger hydraulically hardening mortars can be made from lime. Hydraulic hardening can also take place under water. The great advantage of lime plasters is their very good vapour diffusibility. Lime plasters are alkaline.

The requirements of Mason's lime according to DIN 1061-1. Lime plasters belong to mortar groups P I and P II, according to DIN 18550.

30 Rainfall maps used to calculate the average annual rainfall according to Pörschmann (see also p. 102)
33 Trowel thrown finish as pure lime plaster
34 The old town of Sanaa, Yemen

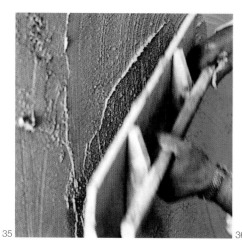

35

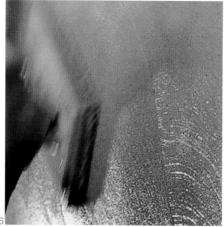

36

Gypsum plasters

Building plasters were standardised in DIN 1168. The new European standard is EN 13279. If gypsum is the active base binder, then the requirements of the mortar are defined here. If non-hydraulic lime is the active base binder, then EN 998 applies. According to the old DIN standard 18550, gypsum plasters belonged to mortar group P IV and the requirements were as for this mortar group. This standard has, however, been replaced by EN 998: 2003. A classification by mortar groups is no longer included in the new standard.

In principle, one can differentiate between gypsum plaster, sand gypsum mortar, gypsum-lime mortar, and lime-gypsum mortar. Each of the gypsum plasters listed has a different mix ratio of gypsum, lime and sand. Gypsum plasters containing loam are also available for purchase. The loam is not used as a binder here, but is an aggregate used to colour the plaster.

The binder in gypsum plaster is mainly gypsum (therefore EN 13279 applies). Building plasters with no additions added by the manufacturer are:
• anhydrous gypsum,
• plaster of Paris (multi-phase gypsum). This begins to stiffen sooner and yet is workable for a longer period of time than anhydrous gypsum.

Building plasters with additions added by the manufacturers contain plaster of Paris, and anhydrous gypsum containing setting agents (retarders, solvents) to achieve certain properties. Three plasters of Paris are listed below:
• machine-applied plaster of Paris (fair-faced plaster), applied using a plaster throwing machine;
• Bond plaster of Paris, for hand plastering on difficult surfaces;

• ready-mix plaster of Paris, for hand plastering.

Gypsum plasters are usually applied in one layer with a thickness of at least 1 cm. If more than one layer is applied then the lower layer must be combed while still fresh. Gypsum plasters contain approx. 20 % chemically bound water by volume. This is the reason for their good fire-resistance (material class A 1). Gypsum plaster can be worked quickly and easily. It is mainly used as machine-applied plaster (fair-faced plaster) in interior spaces. It has the following positive properties: breathable, good capillary force, moisture controlling, low thermal insulation, warm surface, heat retaining, sound-damping, elastic, quick and controlled setting, resistant to insect attack, fire retardant, low manufacturing costs.

Since gypsum is slightly water-soluble, gypsum plaster is only used in interior spaces. It is important that it is not continually exposed to moisture, or it will bloom, become friable and crumble away. Gypsum plaster cannot not be applied to damp brickwork in old buildings without horizontal damp courses. This is because of its open-pored structure with relatively large capillaries, which transport water very quickly. On the other hand, this allows the plaster to dry rapidly. Gypsum plasters set in a few hours or days depending on their composition and harden to a continuous, strong plaster. They do not generally shrink and they remain crack-free. Excess water evaporates so quickly that the surface can be finished soon afterwards. Due to their high water-absorbing capacity, very absorbent plaster bases such as aerated concrete walls, lime sand stone, old brick walls or mixed brickwork must be pre-wetted. If the construction moisture of the building is too high, the plaster

should not be applied until a sufficient drying period has passed, since the plaster will not adhere well to the plaster base if the base is too wet. Weakly absorbent or non-absorbent plaster bases, in particular smooth concrete surfaces, require the use of an adhesion agent.

Gypsum is chemically neutral and not strongly alkaline like cement mortar or concrete, and therefore does not protect steel or iron from rusting. Corrosion will occur if moisture is present. Steel parts should be protected against rusting (with a protective coating, or using galvanised steel parts and Rabitz lathing).

Gauged mortar plaster

Lime-gypsum-sand mixes were used as mortars even in antiquity. The binder here is gypsum and lime. Lime-gypsum plaster has been widely used since the introduction of machine-applied plasters. Today, dry factory-made mortars are generally used, which are suitable for machine application.

Lime protects against attack, gypsum stabilises and stiffens. Pure lime plaster has a low strength. The final strength is increased by adding gypsum. Due to the use of gypsum, these plasters are critical in wet conditions and are therefore used for interior plasterwork, where the surface is usually smoothed or polished. The lime content means that the plaster is caustic during working.

37

38

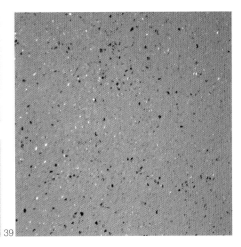
39

Loam mortars

Loam is made up of aluminium silicate (a product of the weathering of stones such as sandstone, clay slate, granite, gneiss, marl or loess) mixed with sand. Loam mortar hardens by the evaporation of water. Bonding is purely mechanical: the fine fractions bond with the sand grains. Loam rendering is a mixture of loam, as a binder, and sands. Plant fibres (wood chippings, straw) can be added as reinforcement. All loams swell when water is added and shrink when they dry, and this can cause cracks to form. The degree of change in volume depends on the clay content and the type of minerals in the clay (kaolinite absorbs little water, montmorillonite swells extensively). Building loam is classified as non-combustible, and is included in material class A 1. Loam rendering has interior climate regulating properties: it takes up moisture from the air and releases it again. It is also heat retaining. It is easy to work and extremely cheap. Further advantages are its anti-allergic properties and its ability to absorb and bind smells (nicotine, cigarette smoke).

Loam mortar is only suitable for use as a base coat plaster or for interior plasterwork. Suitable additions such as dung, fine fibres, casein or a special surface treatment allow the loam mortar also to be used for building elements exposed to rain. Loam rendering is open to diffusion and has a high capillary conductivity, i.e., it must be protected with a suitable finish coat of plaster or paint. Lime plasters from mortar groups P I and some from P II are suitable for use as a finish coat for loam bases, as long as the strength gradient according to the plastering rule is compatible with the loam base coat.

The general rule of plastering, that the strength of the plaster should increase

from the top coat to the base, cannot normally be adhered to for loam plasters, because the protective finish coat is generally harder than the loam base. They should therefore be reinforced, with reed mats, for example.
Loam plaster preserves natural resources and can be recycled by soaking in water. The manufacturing of loam requires only 1 % of the primary energy required to make concrete.

Moist loam causes steel and cast iron to rust. Tiles or coatings that hinder the diffusion of water vapour cannot not be laid on loam. The strength is insufficient in any case. Loam is also unsuitable for use in splash-water areas in wet rooms.

Loam plasters come in many different colours from light ochre to a reddish, dark ochre depending on the area of origin. This creative potential can be expanded by adding various aggregates such as mother-of-pearl or black glass.

Loam mortars are very adhesive; they were formerly preferred for modelling and for overhead work. They can be plastically moulded, can be worked for longer periods of time than setting plastering

40

mortars, and are easy to use without specialist knowledge. Tools and machines do not need to be cleaned very often, since the loam does not set in the machine's tubing. Loam rendering cannot fire-on

35 Gypsum plaster finished by hand
36 Gypsum plaster smoothed with a sponge board
37 Layer structure in a loam plaster system
38 Pigmented loam finish coat
39 Loam surface with black glass aggregate
40 Black glass aggregate

41

Water-resistant plasters / rendering
Water-resistant plasters/rendering are used on the exterior for rain-protection and in the interior in wet rooms. They are not suitable for waterproofing. They reduce the water absorption of the plaster base. The following criterion is valid:
$w \le 2.0 \text{ kg/m}^2\text{h}^{0.5}$
This requirement is fulfilled by lime-cement plasters (MG P I), cement plasters (P III) and also by lime plasters, but the latter only in combination with a lime-cement plaster as a base coat or with admixtures which reduce the uptake of water. Water-repellent properties are achieved by the use of admixtures (AM).

Lime-cement plasters
The mortars in lime-cement plasters contain mason's lime and cement or eminently hydraulic lime as a binder. Mix ratios are laid down in the DIN standards. In the old DIN standard 18550-2, lime-cement plasters were assigned to the mortar group P II b.

Lightweight plasters / rendering
These are a type of lime-cement plaster. If plasters with high compressive strength are applied to lightweight masonry, this goes against the plastering rule. Since today's wall materials are becoming softer and softer due to thermal insulation considerations, there are problems using conventional rendering. In order to ensure sufficient weather resistance of the porous lightweight masonry, rendering is required, which contains a binder with a water-resistant function. The resistance to weather and water increases with an increase in the cement binder content. Cements, however, are stiff, which means that the rendering becomes too hard. Lightweight plasters and rendering that conform to EN 998-1 (formerly DIN 18850-4) have proven themselves in this respect; they are suitable for surfaces

with lower compressive strength. These are ready-mix plasters with a high elasticity and low thermal expansion. Their water-repellent properties are achieved using admixtures. They conformed to the mortar groups P I c and P II in the old DIN standard. They contain mineral aggregates (perlite, expanded clay, frothed glass) or organic light aggregates (expanded polystyrene). These aggregates make them thermally insulating. They should not be confused, however, with thermally insulating plasters.

Trass-lime plasters
Volcanic tuffs contain reactive silicic acid. These include:
1 Pozzoulana and santorin earth; volcanic tuffs already known in antiquity, from Pozzuoli near Naples and from the Greek island of Santorini.
2 Trass, DIN 51 043, ground volcanic stone.

Trass is the best binder due to its resistance to blooming and its durability in moist or wet conditions. Trass-lime plaster is known as the highest quality and most durable plaster and is suitable for all uses. It is more durable than lime and cement plasters, it prevents blooming by binding excess lime insolubly. It also prevents the movement of water required for salt blooming. It is therefore ideal for plastering damp, old brickwork. Overly salinized old brickwork, however, can only be treated by using renovation rendering.

Trass itself does not directly react with water, but only sets slowly, as an exciter, with lime (white lime, hydraulic lime or free lime which is found additionally in cement). Trass lime mortars have a high initial strength and years of afterhardening increase their compressive strength to a level approaching that of cement. This slow development of strength allows

micro cracks, caused by movement of the base material, to be healed. Plasters containing trass harden very slowly, however, and must be kept moist for up to four weeks, which is often seen as a disadvantage during construction.
Trass is added to concrete to make it more dense and durable (by binding the excess lime).

Latent hydraulic materials
Latent hydraulic materials Pozzoulana is regarded as a latent hydraulic additive and is not as finely ground as trass. It reacts slowly with the binder (lime or cement).
This reaction can only take place if lime is present. A cement-like bond is formed in this way. Adding ground brick produces similar properties. The Romans used this reaction to their advantage, ensuring that their harbour structures and bridge foundations hardened to become waterproof, even under water. Vitruvius wrote: "(...) a dusty earth, which by nature has admirable properties, can be found (...) on the mountain of Vesuvius (...)." (Pollio, Marcus Vitruvius, Zehn Bücher über Architektur, Valentin Koerner, Baden-Baden, 1987). The word "trass" comes from the Dutch "Tyrass", meaning "cement".

41 Applying the finish coat plaster by machine
42 Applying cement-lime plaster as a base coat plaster by machine on machine-plastered brickwork

42

Water-repellent plasters/rendering
Plasters and rendering are considered water-repellent if their water absorption coefficient (w-value) is 0.5 kg/m^{2}h$^{0.5}$. The mortar is made water-repellent using hydrophobic admixtures (AM), e. g. oleates, stearates or silicones. The capillary transport of water is lowered such that the plaster/rendering is impervious to capillary water. Water-repellent rendering is used anywhere where the brickwork, or the composite insulation system beneath the plaster, must be protected from moisture.

Cement-lime plasters/rendering
Cement-lime mortars contain cement and hydraulic lime binders, and sand as the aggregate. Hydraulic lime is lime which is dry-slaked in a factory (in a slaking drum with steam) to form a powdered slaked lime.

Cement plaster/rendering is generally stiff and cracks easily. If used as an exterior rendering, the hair cracks soak up water, which can lead to frost damage and damp walls. The vapour permeability and water absorption is low. The addition of lime causes cement plaster to lose its stiffness and strength, since lime is highly elastic. Lime is breathable, moisture controlling and has a good capillary force. The beneficial properties of both binders can be united by mixing them in plaster. Lime plasters, for example, which have a high hydraulic fraction, are more similar to the cement-lime plasters mentioned here in respect of their strength.

Exterior cellar walls, however, are responsible for vertical sealing where they are in contact with the ground. They must be constructed using mortars with hydraulic binders, which react with water to become almost as hard as cement. The water is chemically bound (hydration). The hydrates formed are not soluble in water and therefore protect against water. During the firing of limes that contain clay, compounds are formed from the CaO of the lime and the hydraulic fractions of the clay (silicic acid, SiO$_2$, alumina, Al$_2$O$_3$ and iron oxide, Fe$_2$O$_3$). Hydraulic lime and cement set in the absence of air and produce high strength mortars that harden quickly, but are difficult to work and mould. They absorb only a small amount of moisture from the air compared to building plasters and anhydrite binders, which are easy to work and absorb larger amounts of moisture from the air and are therefore unsuitable for use in wet rooms.

Cement-lime plasters and rendering belong to mortar group P III of the old DIN 18550 standard and have a minimum compressive strength of 10 N/mm^2. (The compressive strength of pure non-hydraulic lime mortar is comparatively very low at 1 N/mm^2.) For older buildings, lightweight masonry or as the finish coat on older plastered surfaces, the compressive strength of cement-lime plaster can be too high. For external plinth rendering it can be reduced from 10 N/mm^2 to 5 N/mm^2, provided that the water-repellent property is assured. In accordance with the plastering rule, the Young's modulus and compressive strength of the rendering must be lower than that of the rendering base. If the rendering is harder than the base, then the rendering will carry the load, where actually the base is intended to carry the load.

Renovation plasters

Renovation plaster systems are used in the renovation of buildings and the preservation of monuments. These are plasters with high porosity and vapour permeability and significantly reduced capillary conductivity.

Renovation plasters are made from premixed dry mortars in accordance with DIN 18557. They have been included in the EN 998-1 standard since September 2003.

Damp brickwork is usually contaminated with salts, which are damaging to building materials. Renovation plasters form bloom-free surfaces on damp brickwork. They have salt-resistant hydraulic binders and are water-repellent. The pores are formed by tensides and light aggregates. The capillaries of the renovation plaster draw the salt solution from the brickwork. The hydrophobe elements in the renovation plaster prevent the salt solution from penetrating the plaster by more than 5 mm. The water evaporates there and reaches the surface of the plaster as water vapour. The salts crystallise in the capillaries and pores of the plaster.

A complete renovation plaster system consists of machine-applied plaster, undercoat, renovation plaster, finish coat and coloured paint. Apart from the renovation plaster, each of the other components may be left out, depending on the case in hand.

The following tests must be carried out before maintenance works can begin:
• Determination of the cause of the damp, and calculation of the moisture equilibrium.
• Determination of the water-soluble salts, which are damaging to building materials, and evaluation of the damag-

ing effect of the salts.
• Determination of the type, and condition of the brickwork with respect to its suitability as a plastering base.

A single-layer renovation plaster system must be at least 2 cm thick. The total thickness of a two-layer renovation plaster system should not be greater than 4 cm. If the undercoat is to serve as a salt trap, it is known as a porous base coat. Equalising and porous base coats are not water repellent. They have a higher porosity and a higher strength than renovation plasters.

According to EN 998-1: 2003 (D) renovation plaster mortar falls into the compressive strength category CS II (1.5 to 5.0 N/mm^2). The capillary uptake of water, c, if used on exterior walls must be c $\geq$ 0.3 kg/m^2 after 24 hours, the water penetration after testing the uptake must be $\leq$ 5 mm, the vapour permeability coefficient $\mu \leq 15$.

Further rising damp is prevented by a borehole seal forming an additional horizontal damp course.

43 Elongated sulphate crystals, which crystallise out in the pore of a renovation plaster (pictures taken in the scanning electron microscope (SEM)).
44 Construction of a renovation plaster system (from left to right)
  a Salinized brickwork with a borehole seal
  b Machine-applied plaster
  c Undercoat
  d Renovation plaster
  e Finish coat
  f Coloured paint
45 Mode of action of a renovation plaster system
46 Application of synthetic resin coating using a smoothing trowel
47 Texturing of the surface with the smoothing trowel

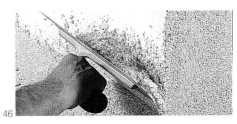
46

47

Synthetic resin plasters
The coating materials of synthetics resin plasters are also subject to monitoring in the same way as factory-made mortars. The required properties must be proven by the manufacturer. This is laid out in DIN 18558.
According to this DIN standard, synthetic resin plasters are coatings which look like plaster. They are made of organic binders and fillers/aggregates in the form of a polymer dispersion or solution. The aggregates are mineral and/or organic, and the majority of the grains are > 0.25 mm. Synthetic resin plasters do not contain inorganic binder fractions such as cement or lime and are therefore not alkaline. They are elastic and are often used on soft surfaces (insulating sheeting). In contrast to mineral plasters, synthetic resin plasters dry only by evaporation of the water or solute fraction. They have a lower pH value, which means that it is possible for algae and mould to grow on their surface. The manufacturers therefore add water-soluble, non-biodegradable biocides. Synthetic resin plasters are supplied ready to use. They are used exclusively as a finish coat with a thickness of 0.5–6.0 mm and require a base coat.

The coating is applied to a base coat of mortar with mineral binders, or directly onto concrete. The base coat plaster must fulfil the terms and requirements defined in EN 998-1, formerly DIN 18550 parts 1 and 2. The synthetic resin coating must be resistant to alkalines, due to the alkaline nature of the base coat plaster. The combination of different skins of plaster is also known as a plaster system in this case.

Table 2 of the DIN standard defines the types of coating materials.
• P Org. 1 Exterior rendering and interior plasterwork
• P Org. 2 Interior plasterwork

Synthetic resin plasters are differentiated by their surface appearance as follows: scraped finish, float finish, ridged finish, spray plaster, coloured stone plaster, modelling plaster and painted plaster. These are imitations of plaster textures. The imitation scraped finish is particularly notable, because approximately one third of the plaster applied in a hand-finished DIN-standard mineral scraped finish is then scraped off again. This way of working is not possible with the thin 5 mm layer of a synthetic resin finish coat.

Silicone resin plasters
These have not been subject to any special standards as yet, i.e., they are not standardised. The binder is a silicone resin emulsion with a small fraction of a polymer dispersion. Further ingredients are pigments, fillers, texturing aggregates and admixtures that improve the workability. The higher filler content means that these plasters can be applied in relatively thick layers. When they have dried, they look similar to mineral plasters. Silicone resin plasters have a high vapour permeability (μ 30–70) and good water-repellent properties. The synthetic resin plasters described above and silicone resin plasters are both assigned to material class B due to their organic binder content. These finish coats are also ready-to-use, paste-like masses, which can be applied to all dry, stable surfaces straight from the pot.

Silicate plasters
Silicate plasters contain potassium water glass as a binder and up to 5 % alkali-resistant polymer dispersion additions. Hardening occurs by the reaction of CO_2 from the air (silification) and by evaporation of the water (see silicate paints, p. 66). Because of their binder, silicate plasters are strongly alkaline and are therefore largely resistant to soiling. The binder is mineral and they are therefore classified as material class A 2. When working with this plaster, alkali-sensitive surfaces (e. g. glass, ceramic, metal) must be masked.

As a result of their high shrinkage factor, potassium water glass bound plasters may only be applied in thin layers. They require a silicating base surface, such as mineral plaster, concrete or fibre cement. They are mainly used on exterior surfaces as a finish coat on lime-cement base coats, but can be used in interior spaces, although not at the base of a wall. In addition, they can be used as a final coat in composite insulation systems. They are noted for their good vapour permeability (μ 5–30), and high resistance to water and acidic materials. They are therefore extremely weather-resistant and have a long service life. On exterior surfaces, potassium water glass bound plasters are often hydrophobed on account of their intrinsic high water absorption. They are also supplied as a ready-to-use paste-like mass.

48

Cement plasters

Cement plasters are made from mortars that make use of Portland cement as the binder and quartz gravel and quartz sand as aggregates. They are stiff and therefore susceptible to cracking, and have only limited water permeability. The mixed plaster is coarse-grained and since it does not contain lime it is difficult to mould.

The aggregate must be dense and compression-proof so that a high packing density can be achieved in the ideal case. These plasters are therefore watertight and resistant to frost damage. DIN 18550 assigns purely cement plasters to mortar group P III b. Their minimum compressive strength is 10 N/mm². Purely cement plasters are water-repellent and impervious to capillary water on account of their composition.

By adding additives, which further increase the density, they can even become impervious to rising water. For these plasters, additional qualification tests are required. Since they are resistant to rising water, they are used as a sealing layer against water. Purely cement mortar plasters are only suitable for use on high strength surfaces and for very abrasion-resistant and splash-water susceptible building elements.

Only pure cement mortars from mortar group III may be used in contact with the soil, for plastering below the damp-proof course, and as a carrier for sealing slurries. This category includes exterior cellar wall plasterwork and exterior plinth rendering. Exterior plinth rendering is continued up to a height of at least 30 cm above ground level. The transition to the lime-cement mortar plasterwork is marked with a trowel joint.

It must be taken into consideration that the strength of the skins of plaster should either be the same, or should decrease somewhat from the base to the top layer. For exterior cellar walls, which have a lower strength than the cement mortar, the compressive strength of the mortar can be reduced from 10 N/mm² to 5 N/mm². In this case, it is imperative that the water-repellent properties of the mortar be ensured by using suitable admixtures. Care should be taken to ensure that there is always a good mechanical bond between the individual layers of plaster, achieved by roughing or felting the base coat plaster.

Cement plasters are also used in interior spaces to plaster wet rooms. According to the old DIN standard 18550, domestic kitchens and bathrooms are not classified as wet rooms.

49

50

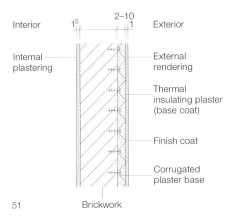

51   Brickwork

2–10

Interior   1,5   ,1   Exterior

Internal   External
plastering   rendering

                                          Thermal
                                          insulating plaster
                                          (base coat)

                                          Finish coat

                                          Corrugated
                                          plaster base

48 Exterior cellar walls with machine-applied plaster
    as a base for cement plaster
49 Window opening, prepared for thermal insulating
    plaster of maximum thickness 12 cm
50 Frothed glass granulate as an aggregate
51 Thermal insulation plaster system on a single-
    shell brick wall with a corrugated plaster base.

Thermal conductivity in comparison
EPS: λ = 0.04 w/(m²K)
Thermal insulating plaster aggregate:
EPS: λ = 0.07 w/(m²K)
Thermal insulating plaster aggregate:
Perlite: λ = 0.08 w/(m²K)
Thermal insulating plaster aggregate:
Perlite + frothed glass: λ = 0.04 w/(m²K)

Required thicknesses, comparison of thermal plasters
with identical U-values, 1.49 W/(m²K)
2.0 cm thermal insulating plaster aggregate: EPS
3.5 cm thermal insulating plaster aggregate: Perlite
6.0 cm thermal insulating plaster aggregate: Perlite +
frothed glass

Plasters for specific uses
Plasters for specific uses were listed in
the DIN standard 18550 part 1. These
are: Thermal insulating plaster, plasters
as fire proofing or with a higher radiation
absorption. Sacrificial, compression, desalting and sound-absorbing plasters are
also listed. The new EN 998-1 standard,
section 3.5.6, classifies thermal insulating
plastering mortars (T) as mortars with
specific thermal insulating properties,
according to the suitability tests.

Thermal insulating plasters
Thermal insulating plasters are mineral-
bound, very light, soft plasters with low
thermal conductivity ($\leq$ 0.2 W/(cm • K)
according to DIN). Thermal insulating
plaster systems are manufactured as a
premixed dry mortar and were subject to
the regulations set down in DIN 18 577
(3) if they had a polystyrene aggregate. If
they contained other aggregates (frothed
glass or perlite), this standard did not
apply. Approval by the building authorities was required.

Thermal insulating plaster forms a seam-
less, homogeneous layer, which is flexible
and levels out any unevenness. It is
always used as a base coat plaster and
must be combined with a finish coat plaster to protect it from mechanical damage
and weathering. In the ideal case, a stippled finish is used.
According to DIN standards, the following
applies:
base coat plaster:
d = min. 20 mm – max. 100 mm
finish coat:
d = min. 8 mm – max. 15 mm

Finish coats are generally harder than
thermal insulating base coats. The plastering rule, that the plaster should not be
harder than the base material, does not
apply here. This works, as long as the fin-

ish coat is not too thick and the compressive strength of the finish coat does not
exceed certain limits. The two layers must
be designed to be perfectly compatible.
As well as for improving thermal insulation, thermal insulating plaster is also
used on particularly difficult surfaces. As
a light plaster base coat, it reduces the
susceptibility to cracking by uncoupling
the finish coat and the brickwork. For this
reason, insulating plaster systems ideally
compliment lightweight masonry, for
example, serving as a capillary, mineral
skin of plaster that is open to diffusion.

Sacrificial plasters
These plasters draw salts out from damp
brickwork and are then removed (sacri-
ficed) after 1 to 2 years depending on
their saturation. Sacrificial and compression plasters should not be confused with
renovation plasters. They do not contain
salt-resistant binders and are not water-
repellent. Quite the opposite - they are
usually very porous, capillary-action, car-
bonitically-bound mortar groups. Their
low strength is necessary in order to ease
their removal after desalting, without damaging the treated surface. There are no
guidelines covering renovation plasters,
therefore the purpose of their use should
be considered on a case by case basis.
Good customer advice should make it
clear that sacrificial plaster has a short life
and that its removal is part of the renovation process. If sacrificial plaster is not
removed, there is a danger that the salinized plaster will remain on the brickwork
for too long. The protection of the brickwork is then no longer guaranteed.

52

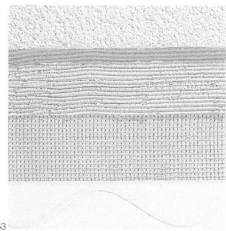
53

External thermal insulation composite systems (ETICS)

Composite insulation systems have been on the market since about 1970. These systems are based on the principle that specific, compatible materials are "bonded" together and attached to the brickwork as a package to improve insulation. Composite insulation systems consist of at least three layers:
• thermal insulating layer,
• reinforcing layer, plaster mass and embedded plaster mesh,
• final coat, weather protection.

There are no standards for these systems; the individual components are subject to approval by the building authorities. Accordingly, only closed systems may be used. Mixed systems using third-party components are not covered by the manufacturer's guarantee.

The most common ETICS systems are:
• rigid foam sheeting (polystyrene or polyurethane) with a mineral plaster system or synthetic resin / silicone plasters
• mineral fibre insulating materials with a mineral plaster system
• cork insulating sheets with a mineral plaster system
• reed insulating sheets with a mineral plaster system

The insulating elements are fixed directly to a load-bearing surface using adhesive, or are anchored using insulation fasteners. Since heat bridges are then formed, depending on the material, screws with plastic heads must be used. If the surface is very uneven and has no load-bearing capacity, rail systems are often used, so that the existing surface material need not be removed or pre-treated.

As part of the exterior wall construction, the ETICS system is subject to local building regulations. These require, among other things, the following fire protection ratings:
• Building at least ≤ 2 full storeys
  class B 2 (normal flammable)
• Building > 2 full storeys
  class B 1 (flame resistant)
• high-rise building, building > 22 m in height
  class A (non-flammable)

Due to the requirements of the fire regulations, mineral wool sheets are often used as insulation. They are incombustible (belong to material class A 1), their corners and edges are stable and they are dimensionally exact.
Mineral foam (calcium silicate) sheets are also in common use. They are made of inorganic components, quartz meal (sand), hydraulic lime and cement. They are completely free of fibres, incombustible, and open to diffusion.
Perimeter plates are used at the base of buildings. These are rigid foam sheets with a higher resistance to mechanical loading from the pressure of the soil and which are insensitive to spray water.

Insulating materials made from polystyrene, timber, cork or reed are assigned to either material class B 1 or B 2. Plasters with organic binders are generally classed as class B 1 materials; silicate and mineral plasters as class A. ETICS systems with mineral fibre insulation and a final coat of synthetic resin plaster are also considered class B 1 materials.

The ETICS system must be self-supporting and able to absorb the force of the wind. Changes in temperature and vapour pressure have a significant effect on the system. The formation of condensation on the surface of the building ele-ment or within the ETICS system itself must be prevented. Dew point calculations are required at an early stage, therefore, to determine the required thickness of the insulating material layers. In addition, the system must be adequately protected from driving rain with a water-repellent rendering.

It should not be forgotten that the installation of an ETICS system on a heat-retaining solid construction will result in less solar energy being absorbed. The system cools down in the evening and moisture from the surrounding air can condense on the cold facade, causing condensation.

52 Construction of an ETICS system with mineral wool insulation
    Mineral wool sheets
    Reinforcing woven material
    Reinforcing mortar
    Covering coat
53 Layer system of a ETICS system with rigid foam insulation
    Rigid foam insulation
    Reinforcing woven material
    Reinforcing mortar
    Covering coat
54 Hammer screw; the colours indicate the different lengths, outside right: an insulation fastener
55 Screw dowel
56 Insulation disk
57 Anchoring depths

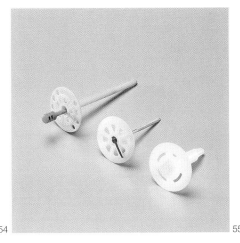

54

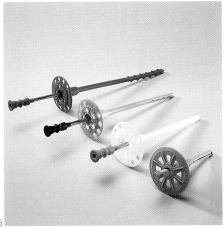

55

56

Depending on the base surface, the type of insulation and the height of the building, different fastening systems can be used to fix the ETICS system. The simplest and cheapest method is using adhesives. A suitable surface should be strong, dry, and free of dust and grease. The abrasion resistance of the surface should be at least 0.08 N/mm. The more uneven the background, e.g. in older buildings or renovation projects, the more likely it is that the insulation blocks must also be mechanically fixed. Some materials, e.g. mineral wool sheets, require additional securing independent of the condition of the surface. This is provided using dowels/plugs and/or rails. If the unevenness in the facade is less than 1.0 cm in the vertical, ETICS systems can be fixed in place using adhesives. This is also approved for buildings less than 8.0 m in height. If the unevenness of the facade is greater than 2.0 cm, the insulating material must be affixed using plugs/dowels in addition to the adhesive. Above 3.0 cm of unevenness, additional rail systems are required. In buildings between 20.0 and 100.0 m tall, a stability check must be carried out for the insulation system. A matrix of the systems cannot be

compiled, since decisions must always be made on a case-by-case basis depending on the insulation material used, the condition of the background and the height of the building. Only plugs/dowels approved by the building regulation authorities may be used as fasteners. These are marked as such by the manufacturers. If dowels/plugs are used, which are not approved for use with that particular system, then the guarantee and therefore also the manufacturer's liability for the entire system expire.

The different types of fasteners are named according to their mounting method, e.g. screw dowels and hammer screws, and also according to their use: insulation fasteners or mounting screws. The edge and axis distances and the minimum component thickness are defined for fasteners with building regulation approval. For standard fasteners, the edge distance is generally twice the anchoring depth (hv) and the axis distance is approximately four times hv. 4–6 fasteners/m² are required in the surface, more at the edge. The anchoring depth is the distance between the surface of the bearing material and the lower edge of

the fastener head (see fig. 57). The bore hole must be at least 10–15 mm deeper than the anchoring depth to allow the screw to penetrate the end of the plug and take up the drill dust. The maximum bearing length depends on the thickness of the insulation, the adhesive layer and any non-load bearing old layers. The length of the fasteners varies from 75 to 340 mm. They are used in a bolted construction. The insulation or the rail is drilled with the same diameter hole as the surface material.

Hammer screw: Suitable for use with all surfaces and available in lengths from 55–275 mm and in special lengths. The pre-assembled screw is inserted into the load-bearing surface after drilling, and the expanding nail is hammered home.
Screw dowel: Suitable for use with all surfaces and available in lengths from 105–425 mm and in special lengths. The pre-assembled dowel is inserted into the bearing surface material after drilling and the screw is tightened.
Drilled or fixing fasteners: Generally suitable for use with solid surfaces and available in lengths from 50–180 mm and in special lengths. No pre-drilling is necessary: the pre-assembled fastener is inserted into the surface and pulled tight in one operation.
Insulation fasteners: Especially for mineral wool, insulation fasteners with a diameter d = 140 mm are used instead of the usual d = 60 mm, to give better load distribution.
Insulation or installation fasteners: For light loads, special plastic fasteners can be used. Lamps, for example, can be mounted onto these using particle board screws. For heavier loads, special thermally-uncoupled subconstructions can be used.

Old layers of plaster   Thickness of insulation

Adhesive layer

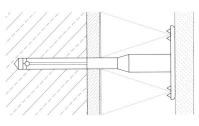

h_v = Anchoring depth   Useful length

t = Drill hole depth

57

Table 58

Anchoring surface	t	hv
Solid materials	≤ 60 mm	≤ 50 mm
Aerated concrete	≤ 120 mm	≤ 110 mm
Solid and porous materials	≤ 80 mm	≤ 70 mm
Concrete	≤ 60 mm	≤ 50 mm

Fastener

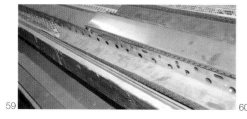

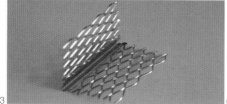

Plaster rails

The term "plaster rails" includes a wide variety of shaped sections, corner angles and bandings. They are used to protect areas particularly susceptible to damage such as corners or jambs, to stabilise thick layers of plaster and to form expansion joints or drip heads on balconies and plinths. They also help in making the plaster surface even and geometrically exact. Some examples are:

• Wire angle
• Edge trims
• Interior edge trims
• Screed rails
• Plasterwork edge trims
• Plasterwork joint trims
• Wall base and lintel sections
• Drip rails
• Expansion joint sections
• Movement joint sections
• Jamb edge and covering sections
• Hangers and connecting sections for composite insulation systems

The dimensions of the rails depend on the thickness of the plaster and their intended use. For interior plasterwork, a filler coat of 15 to 1 mm is assumed. For exterior rendering, a thermal insulating plaster layer of 20 to 60 mm is assumed. Projections of up to 160 mm are required for the mounting rails of ETICS systems. The rails are usually available in 3 m lengths, but they are also available in special lengths.

They are made of special steel, aluminium, galvanised steel or plastic. The galvanised steel sheet is drawn or punched. This gives the sections their typical shape, which guarantees the shape of the indenting and the bond with the plastering or rendering mortar. Galvanised rails are usually used in plastering or rendering systems, and plastic corner angles with glued-on woven material strips are normally used with ETIC systems. Galva-nised sections may not be used in conjunction with the commonly used plastic-modified top coatings, since the zinc layer will be attacked. Stainless steel sections are recommended for exterior use, for wet rooms and for renovation plasters. To achieve very smooth, even surfaces, rails are used not only at the corners and edges, but also in the middle of the surface. The laths are fixed to the wall, at distances of about 1.0 m, and adjusted. The plaster is then applied and smoothed and the rails are removed again. This particularly high-quality finish is traditionally known as "Plaster with Parisian laths", although timber laths were formerly used. These can still be used today; the edges of the plaster will then be softer. Plasterwork can also be carried out without using rails at the edges, of course. This is particularly useful in renovation work.

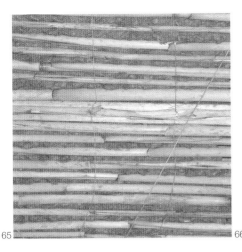

65   66   67

Plastering/rendering bases

The plastering/rendering base is the building element to be plastered/rendered. The properties of rendering bases are regulated in DIN 18350. According to VOB part C (DIN 18359), the condition of the surface to be plastered/rendered must be checked before the plaster, rendering or coating is applied. This can be a visual inspection or can take the form of wiping, scratching or wetting tests.

The stability of the base, with which the plaster or rendering must form a strong, lasting bond, is important for the quality and service life of the plasterwork or rendering. The suitability of the plaster/rendering base to be plastered/rendered is to be checked with great care.

The strength of the layers which form the wall should decrease from the wall to the outer surface. The choice of a particular plastering or rendering system depends on the final strength of the plastering or rendering mortar and on the strength and absorption capacity of the base. The base must have adequate strength and be free of dust. There should be no friable components.

Strongly absorbent bases should be adequately wetted, especially when using lime mortars, for example, to promote slow, continuous hardening and prevent firing-on. Alternatively, the base can be pre-treated with a machine-applied plaster. This machine-applied plaster is not part of the plaster or rendering system, but is classed as part of the wall. It is applied as a semi-covering "net" and should not form a closed covering sealing layer (coverage < 50%). Its purpose is to improve bonding to the base.

Lathwork

Lathwork is used when building elements do not constitute a suitable base for the proposed plaster or rendering system, either because they have insufficient strength (lightweight masonry, ETIC systems) or they cannot form a strong bond with the mortar (timber or steel elements).

The base is completely covered with a net-like or perforated covering made of alkali-resistant material. The covering is intended to improve the bonding of the plaster or rendering. The plaster or rendering system then becomes largely independent of the load-bearing construction. It must be ensured that the plaster or rendering remains crack-free, strong and dimensionally stable, even when there is no bonding with the load-bearing construction. The following are used as lathwork, e.g.:
• Wire mesh (Rabitz lathing)
• Brick wire mesh
• Rib mesh
• Plastic or glass fibre mesh
• Reed mats.
  (The requirements were formerly regulated by DIN 18550).
• Timber mats

The lathwork, nails and brackets used must be protected from rust if used with gypsum or loam, or in wet rooms (use galvanised fasteners).

59 Rails and mesh angles
60 Exterior render section, stainless steel perforated sheet
61 Drip heads, aluminium
62 Fasteners and joint rails for composite insulation systems, aluminium
63 Interior plasterwork section, galvanised expanded metal
64 Wire angle, stainless steel
65 Reed mats as lathwork in a renovation project
66 Loam bricks with galvanised wire meshing
67 Plastic mesh
68 Brick wire mesh

68

69

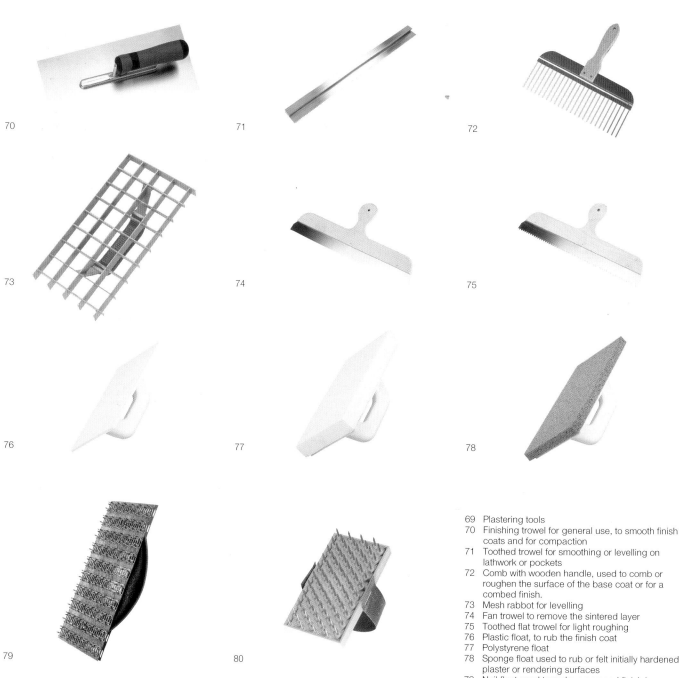

70

71

72

73

74

75

76

77

78

79

80

69 Plastering tools
70 Finishing trowel for general use, to smooth finish coats and for compaction
71 Toothed trowel for smoothing or levelling on lathwork or pockets
72 Comb with wooden handle, used to comb or roughen the surface of the base coat or for a combed finish.
73 Mesh rabbot for levelling
74 Fan trowel to remove the sintered layer
75 Toothed flat trowel for light roughing
76 Plastic float, to rub the finish coat
77 Polystyrene float
78 Sponge float used to rub or felt initially hardened plaster or rendering surfaces
79 Nail float used to make a scraped finish by scraping off the hardened top layer
80 Comb to texture the surface

Rendering and plaster surfaces can be decorated in many ways, with regard to both colour and texture, thanks to their good moulding properties. There used to be many individual styles thanks to the different regional building traditions, but these are disappearing due to increasing use of machines.

The textured finish is generally independent of the type of mortar used. The following possibilities exist for texturing:

- by using different types of aggregates (grain size, grain shape, colour) in the plaster/render
- by the way in which the plaster/render is applied
- by throwing on, applying with a trowel, machine application, etc. The texture produced is dependent on the skilled use of the tool or machine,
- by manual application: the "signature" of the craftsman can be seen in the surface, since every craftsman uses a slightly different throwing technique,
- by treating the surface of the fresh plaster/render, e. g. by wiping, combing, scratching, or revealing the aggregate by washing away the binder,
- by masonry works to the already hardened mortar on the wall,
- by using coloured pigments.

The different ways of working the surface of the finish coat or coloured rendering/plaster are known as plastering methods. The most important methods are listed below:
Decorative mortar techniques are: scratching, cutting, intarsia and sgraffito, which allow both positive and negative reliefs to be produced.

Sgraffito

The name of this technique comes from the Italian and means "to scratch". Sgraffito is a picture made my scratching lines or areas into a multi-layered coloured plaster. The plaster consists of a base coat, scratchwork and scratch coat. The picture is formed in lime plaster made with sharp fluvial sand. The scratchwork is made up of individual layers of coloured lime plaster, approximately 4 mm thick, applied wet-in-wet on top of each other. The plaster can be coloured with charcoal, with pigments which have been soaked overnight, or with ground aggregates such as schist, basalt, marble etc. The moist finish coat can be painted al fresco or with casein paints. Lines or areas are scratched with an angled cut from the finish coat using angled knives, curls, scrapers or spikes. The angled cut prevents the edges from weathering. The construction must be planned and worked in daily steps.

Stuccolustro

(smoothed fresco, also known as Pompeian wall painting) The smoothing of the fresh surface of a fresco to achieve a glossy marbled finish was known in antiquity. After the application of a machine-sprayed coat, a base coat and a compacted layer of fresh lime mortar as an intermediate layer, and three layers of fresco, approximately 1 cm thick in total, are applied. The third layer is a fine marble mortar made from pigmented lime putty, which is smoothed and waxed using a heated stainless steel trowel after hardening. The quality of the smoothness of the surface, the shine and the wipe-resistance can be improved by using olive oil or soapy water. The temperature, start and duration of the smoothing process are determined by experience. Stuccolustro can be used as high-quality exterior rendering.

Scrubbed plaster

In this technique, the aggregates in the plaster are made visible by washing or scrubbing out the not yet hardened binder slurry from the surface. The surface is scrubbed with a brush until the grains protrude clearly. The grains should not be scrubbed out, however. The remaining cement film is removed as the last step. Naturally coloured aggregates (e.g. split brick, coloured glass and coloured gravel) and pigmented lime-cement mortars offer a range of decorative possibilities. DIN 18550 part 2 demands the use of large grained aggregates. The base coat must be to MG III standard. This ensures that it is particularly resistant to knocks and suitable for high moisture environments. The coarse, heavy grain requires a high bonding force. Pure lime is not sufficient; an additional hydraulic binder is necessary.

81　Trowel-thrown plaster as a purely lime plaster, rough texture: pit lime, smooth texture: lime trass mortar, brushed, Bernhardskapelle, 2002, architect: Hans Klumpp
82　Stuccolustro
83　Sgraffito
84　Scrubbed plaster with glass brick, pale coloured
85　Scrubbed plaster with glass brick, dark coloured

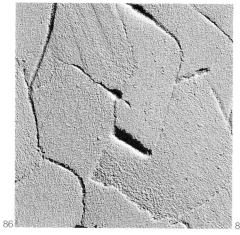

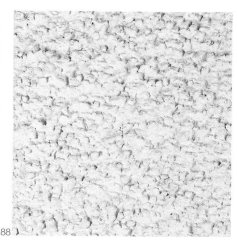

Trowelled plaster

This is one of the finer textured plasters with regard to the aggregates (grain sizes: fine 0.3–2.5 mm). The thrown-on and slightly hardened mortar is compacted using a smoothing trowel. The trowelling marks remain visible, they can be horizontal, vertical, arched, fanned or scaled. The origin of this technique can be traced back to the middle ages. The thrown-on or manually applied mortar was smoothed with a trowel. The technique of smoothing a white lime hydrate slurry into the surface as part of the same operation, (forming a chemical bond between the plaster and the paint), also stems from this period. This results in an even, slightly undulating and hilly plaster finish, influenced by the unevenness of the brickwork. Quadratic, triangular and smoothing trowels with rounded edges are used to achieve this surface finish. Different styles:
• Fan or scale-shaped, heavily textured with uniform or changing trowel marks.
• Slightly scrubbed
• Decorative striped or ribbed structure

Felted or smoothed plaster

Shortly before the plaster hardens, the surface is rubbed with a soft felt or sponge disc, or a smoothing trowel. A very fine, compacted surface is achieved (grain size: fine 0.3 – coarse 2.5 mm) with the same consistency as trowelled plaster, though more finely finished. Because of its modest texture, the quality of the material is significant for this finish coat, e.g. loam and lime plasters. Today, only rougher base coats are felted. The finish coat is usually smoothed using a sponge board, since additives necessary for processing the material make it too sticky to be smoothed with a felt disc.
Different styles:
• combed rendering
  The fine grained finish coat is combed horizontally, vertically or in different directions while fresh, using a toothed trowel or a steel or wooden comb (art nouveau style plaster).
• Stamp and roller plaster
  These are finely grained but applied thickly using wooden, rubber, leather or metal stamps and rollers to press in three dimensional textures, patterns or ornaments.

Trowel thrown plasters

The structure is achieved by throwing the plaster onto the surface using a trowel. Generally, coarse aggregates (grain size: fine 6 – coarse 12 mm) are used.
These plasters are some of the oldest textured plasters to be applied by craftsmen. The rough surface texture is dependent on the grain size and the skill of the plasterer. His throwing-on technique, in particular, can result in different coarse and fine textures. The force, with which the mortar is thrown onto the machine-applied plaster or base coat, ensures a good bond.
Different styles:
• Thrown-on trowel plaster, thrown-on mortar remains in place,
• Brushed thrown-on trowel plaster, the thrown-on mortar is brushed lightly,
• Trowelled spray plaster, spraying of liquid mortar with large, rounded aggregate grains (also trowel thrown plaster with ballast (3–16 mm).
• Slap dash, protruding areas are picked up with the edge of the trowel and thrown into any valleys in the mortar,
• Rustic plaster, after throwing-on and rough levelling, a wet float is pressed into the surface and pulled off with a jerk.
• butted, stippled using a brushwood brush.

86 trowelled plaster, modelled
87 felted plaster
88 trowel thrown plaster
89 trowelled plaster, smoothed
90 combed plaster (art nouveau style) structured using a comb
91 spray plaster
92 Munich plaster
93 scraped finish
94 rubbed-finish rendering

91

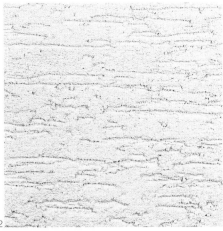

92

93

Spray plaster
The sprayed application of a fine-grained, thin liquid mortar produces an even, grainy texture which can be altered by varying the grain size of the aggregate (grain size: fine 1.5–coarse 4.0 mm). The fine grain size and thin liquid are optimal parameters for machine application. Today they are usually applied in two or more sprayed layers using plaster spraying machines. The use of plaster spraying machines makes spray plaster a very cheap and therefore widely used finish coat. This plaster was formerly known as broom finished plaster, the oldest type of plaster finish. A brushwood brush was dipped in mortar and rapped against a wooden pole on the wall, causing the mortar to spray onto the still fresh, rubbed base coat. This principle of forming a good bond using the wet, chemically active base coat leads to the formation of a strong spray plaster.

Polished textured plasters, rubbed-finish rendering The texture is produced by the coarsest grains when rubbing the surface.
The grain size used is: fine 1.5–coarse 5 mm, and special grades up to 7 mm. The grain is rubbed against the fresh finish coat and results in grooves being formed. The tool used is a wooden board. The following styles can be used:
· Munich plaster, horizontal rubbing,
· Vermicular finish, circular rubbing,
· Bark or drag finish, vertically drawn with a trowel,
· Old German rendering, rubbed with a wooden board in all directions, and other types.

Scraped finishes
These can only be used on mineral lime or cement binders. They are applied in a layer 10–15 mm thick depending on the coarsest grade of the aggregate. The grain sizes used today range from 1–9 mm, depending on the required ease of use with a machine. If the plaster is manually applied, grain sizes of up to 16 mm are possible. Scraped finish plasters must be applied more thickly – up to 3–4 times their grain size – than other plasters. After a suitable hardening period, the binder-rich surface is scratched away to a depth of 8–10 mm using a nail float. This produces a greater surface area and shrinkage cracking is prevented. If a single-coat system is used, a total thickness of 20–25 mm is necessary. The characteristic texture is formed by the protrusion of round or broken grains. Mineral scraped finish plasters may sand, depending on the material. According to DIN 18550, this does not constitute a material defect. The grains that sand off take with them dirt, germs and spore, removing them from the facade. The rough surface means that rain water runs down the facade more slowly. The water disperses throughout the material by means of capillary forces and is not concentrated at the open surface. This prevents too much algae from growing. The rendering can retain its own colour without the need for paint. It can only be cleaned using high pressure water.

94

Masonry-worked rendering
The rendering base must be resistant to compression and knocks. To enable masonry works such as chiselling or pointing to be carried out on the hardened rendering, the aggregates must be of low to medium strength, e.g. sandy limestone, shell lime or marble granulate.

Paints and coatings

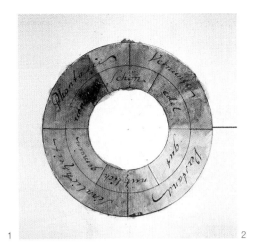

Isidore of Seville (560–636), scholar in the early middle ages described paint as "captured sunlight". 1400 years later, the German DIN standard describes the measurement of colour as follows: "Colour is the property of an area in the field of view that seems to have no structure and which allows this area to be differentiated, on viewing with one unmoving eye, from a similar structureless area bordering on the original and seen at the same moment."

The discussion as to whether our perception of colour is subjective or objective is an old one. Sir Isaac Newton tried to order the colours of the rainbow into a linear, measurable spectrum. Goethe was a little less scientific in developing his own colour circle from his theories on the polarity of light and darkness (see figs. 1, 2).

Paint as a building material
Colours in all shades of the rainbow are used to decorate buildings. Paint does not, however, simply add colour, but is also a structural component, providing protection against the weather, moisture and water, and against atmospheric, chemical, biological, mechanical or other influencing factors. In addition, paint has a decorative element. In German, the same word, Farbe, is used for both colour and paint, demonstrating the strong relationship between the two concepts. In this part of the book we present the basic principles necessary to evaluate the characteristics of today's commonly-used coating systems for rendered facades and for common building materials, and to select them for specific uses (depending on the surface to be coated).

Coatings – a definition
The term "coating", which includes the traditional terms paint, varnish and lacquer, today also includes a large number of protective systems including filling

compounds and floor coatings. Coating materials as defined in DIN 55945 – paints and varnishes – are liquid to pasty, or powdered materials, which consist of binders, pigments or other colouring matters, fillers, solvents and other ingredients.

There is more than one way of classifying and describing paints. Colloquially the function of the paint is often used as a descriptor: fire-retardant paint, anticorrosive paint, wood paint or house paint. They are also classified as either primer or top coat. The surface to be painted is also used as a necessary means of distinct classification; wood, steel, mineral materials. The most obvious classification, as for plaster and rendering systems, is by binder, e. g. alkyd varnishes for their alkyd binders or silicate paints for their potassium water glass base, as these are responsible for the adhesion of the paint to the surface. Almost all products sold under trade names can today be classified and evaluated based on binder type.

Physical properties of paints
The adhesion of a coating material to a surface is not the only important criterion by which it is selected, but also and primarily the physical properties of the coating and their suitability in combination with the surface to be coated. It is this combination that ensures the coating system has a long life and is physically effective. For this reason, the European Standard for coating materials, prEN 1062, uses these physical properties as a means of classification.
Paints are differentiated by the following properties:
• Water vapour diffusion current density – see Appendix, table of paint classes (p. 105),
• Liquid water transmission – see Appen-

dix, table of paint classes (p. 105)
• Carbon dioxide permeability – see Appendix, table of paint classes (p. 105),
• Sheen – shiny, medium, matt,
• Thickness of layer (< 50 µm to > 400 µm),
• Grain size – fine, medium, coarse, very coarse,
• Crack bridging – no requirements to > 2500 µm.

1   Colour circle "Representation of the human mind and soul", J. W. von Goethe, 1809
2   Spectral colours created, for example, by the refraction of sunlight

3 4 5

To minimise moisture-related damage to facades, the absorption of water, e.g. from rain or condensation, must be in equilibrium with the drying which follows. This water equilibrium can be characterised for coatings using the parameters outlined below.

Absorption of water
The more water a coating absorbs, the more water ends up in the surface beneath it. Plaster or rendering becomes damp and peels on exposure to frost, or algae or mould grows. Timber becomes mouldy, metal rusts. The absorption of water is given as the water absorption coefficient; the amount of water absorbed in 24 hours is noted as weight absorbed per unit area and unit time: $kg/(m^2h^{0.5})$. A

high water absorption is more than 0.5 kg, a low water absorption less than 0.1 kg.

Water vapour diffusion
Water that enters the structure should evaporate again as soon as possible, especially in absorbent surfaces such as house paints or wood coatings. The ability for water to evaporate is measured by the sd-value, the µ-value and the V-value. The sd-value describes the resistance to the diffusion of water vapour. The lower the s_d-value, the more permeable is the coating. The µ-value or water vapour diffusion resistance coefficient is the unitless quotient of the s_d-value (m) and the thickness of the coating $\mu = s_d/d$ (g/cm^2). The water vapour diffusion cur-

rent density, the V-value in $g/(m^2d)$ (see Appendix, table of paint classes, p. 105), quantifies how much water vapour can diffuse through a surface in a particular time. The greater the V-value, the more permeable the coating is by water vapour. 150 g is considered a high and 15 g a low current density.

Carbon dioxide permeability
To prevent excessive carbonatisation of the steel in concrete units, they should be treated with a coating impervious to CO_2. The s_d-value (CO_2) is calculated in the same way as the water vapour resistance. The higher this value is, the more impervious the coating is to CO_2.

Table 6 Paint properties

	Binders	Solidification/ hardening	Water absorption coefficient w in $kg/m^2h^{0.5}$	Resistance to the diffusion of water vapour μH_2O	Water vapour permeability s_d in m	CO_2 permeability s_d in m
Calcimine	Hydraulic lime	Chemical hardening/ carbonation	> 1.0 permeable by water	< 10	< 0.1 m (0.02) permeable by water vapour	< 0.5 m
Silicate paint	Potassium water glass	Physical drying/ chemical hardening, silification	> 1.0 permeable by water	< 10	< 0.1 m (0.04–0.08) permeable by water vapour	< 0.5 m
Emulsion-type silicate paint	Potassium water glass/ polymer emulsion	Physical drying/ chemical hardening, silification	0.1–2.0 water resistant	100–1000	0.1–0,5 m (0.08–0.6) permeable by water vapour	< 0.5 m
			0.1–0.5 water repellent	100–1000	0.1–2.0 m permeable by water vapour	< 0.5 m
Polymer emulsion paint	Polymer emulsion	Physical drying/ coalescence	0.1–2.0 water resistant	1000	0.1–1.5 m permeable by water vapour	1–5 m to > 50 m
			0.1–0.5 water repellent	1000	0.1–2.0 m permeable by water vapour	
Silicone resin emulsion paint	Silicone resin emulsion polymer emulsion	Physical drying/ coalescence	< 0.1 watertight	100–1000	< 0.1 m permeable by water vapour	< 0.5 m
Polymerisate resin paint	Synthetic resin	Physical drying/ coalescence	0.1–2.0 water repellent	1000–10 000	0.5–1.0 m water vapour retarding	> 50 m
			0.1–2.0 water repellent	1000–10 000	0.1–2.0 m water vapour retarding	
Hydrophobing agent	Silicone resin	Physical drying/ coalescence	< 0.1 watertight		< 0.1 m permeable by water vapour	> 50 m

7

8

9

Paint ingredients

Paints, or coatings in general, consist of binders, solvents, fillers, pigments and auxiliary substances. These ingredients, which are added and mixed in the solid or liquid state, determine the colour and above all the properties of the paint. During the middle to end of the last century they were often mixed and stirred by the craftsmen themselves. Today, however, most paints used are delivered ready-mixed directly from the paint manufacturer to the construction site (see fig. 9).

Binders

These belong to the non-volatile ingredients in the paint and are responsible for the bonding to the various surfaces. Binders are either liquid in their natural state (e.g. linseed oil) or are solutions of solid materials (e.g. natural or synthetic resins). As the binder hardens or the solvent evaporates, the pigments become "glued" together and to the surface. Binders can be divided, according to their origins, into vegetable, mineral, animal and synthetic binders. PrEN 1062 lists the following binder groups:
acrylic resin, alkyd resin, bitumen, cement, chlorinated rubber, epoxy resin, slaked lime, oil, polyester, water glass, silicone resin, polyurethane, vinyl resin.

A further classification of the binders, and therefore the paints, is by the solution state or the state of dispersion and the resulting hardening of the coating.

Solvents

Solvents are used to dissolve solid binders, which are necessary to ensure that the paint bonds with the surface being coated. They can be split into two groups: aqueous binders and binders that contain organic solvents such as ethanol or benzine. Emissions from organic solvents catch fire easily, are sometimes poisonous and can be detrimental to health. For this reason, aqueous solutions have been developed in recent decades for almost all applications. They are also used, for example, in emulsion and silicate paints. A further development are the low-solvent (high-solid) or solvent-free coatings, e.g. liquid resins. This group includes silicone rubber for seams and polyurethane foams or floor coverings based on polyurethane or epoxy resins. In these substances, known as total-solid coatings, there is no evaporation process - they are moisture-curing.

Colouring matters

Colouring matters are divided into pigments and dies and determine the colour of the paint. Inorganic or organic pigments, which are insoluble in both binder and solvent, are most frequently used. They disperse in the binder and are responsible for colour and coverage. Ground sil or red bole and chalk are natural inorganic, and indigo and umber natural organic pigments. Some pigments also provide protection against corrosion or UV light. Dies, in contrast, are almost exclusively organic, e.g. from the madder root, and are soluble in the medium used. They seem transparent and are used in scumble glazes and for textiles. The compatibility with the binder must be taken into account for all pigments (cement-fast, lime-fast).

Fillers

Fillers also belong to the colouring ingredients, although they only slightly influence the final colour. These are mostly fine stone meals which lend the pigments and dies body, volume and hardness, especially in exterior house paints. They are also insoluble and help reduce costs by reducing the quantity of pigment required.

Auxiliary substance

Additive auxiliary substances or additives, included in small quantities, improve certain properties e.g. the shelf life, workability or appearance.

3 Inorganic coloured pigments
4 Mineral fillers
5 Talc as a filler
6 Paint properties
7 Paint room
8 Pit lime binder
9 Industrial manufacturing of emulsion paints

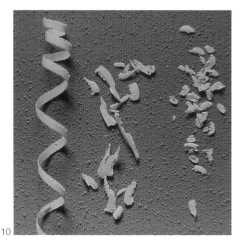

10

a   Emulsion paint, bonds to the surface by adhesion, coalescence
b   Silicone resin emulsion paint, bonds to the surface by adhesion, porous coalescence due to addition of silicon
c   Silicate paints, bonds to the surface by silification, no coalescence
d   Emulsion-type silicate paint, bonds to the surface by silification and adhesion ("gluing") of the respective components, no coalescence
e   Varnish, bonds to the surface by adhesion coalescence
f   Two-component coatings bond to the surface by adhesion, coalescence

1	Coloured pigments	6	Silification
2	Polymer emulsion	7	Binders
3	Adhesive effect	8	Curing agent
4	Solvents	9	Surface
5	Silicon		

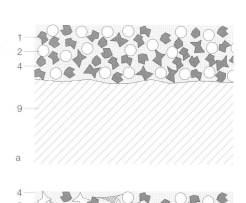

a

b

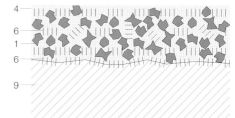

c

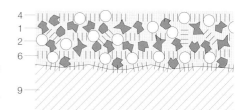

d

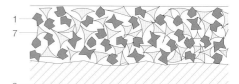

e

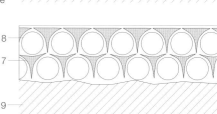

f

11

Coating systems

Paint finishes are mostly multi-layer and are therefore known as coating systems. Often, the surface is additionally treated, e. g. to achieve better adhesion or to prevent excess absorption. Analogous to plastering/rendering systems, the strength of the outer layers should be lower than that of the layers beneath to prevent cracks forming due to stresses between the different layers.

The primer or base coat consists of one or two layers of paint. The top coat is one or more layers of paint, depending on the coverage, and is known as the intermediate coat or finish coat. Multiple thin coats require increased effort, but dry better and produce a more even end result. Where several coating systems are used on top of one another, e. g. in renovation work, this decreases the physical properties of the paints as well as the vapour permeability and increases the stresses, and should therefore by avoided.

The thickness of a coat is usually given in Ìm (micrometres), in mm for floor coatings and in l/m2 for absorbent surfaces, e. g. using deep primer.

Coatings can be applied as transparent (clear) coats, scumbling (where the background can be seen through the coating) or opaque coats (complete coverage). They can be applied industrially, e. g. dipping, spray-coating or powder-coating of metals, or manually, with brushes, rollers, sponges or trowels. Depending on the tool used to apply the coating, the finished result can be anything from smooth to textured.

Drying, hardening, coalescence

The properties of paints are influenced by their hardening process, which is determined by the binder in the paint. This is present, together with the other ingredients, either as an aqueous solution or dissolved in an organic solvent. The following types of hardening can occur:
• Physical drying, in which a film is formed by the evaporation of the solvent, e. g. by the evaporation of water in emulsion paints or the evaporation of organic solvents in polymerisate paints.
• Purely chemical hardening with only a small amount of, or no, solvent (only < 5 % by volume). This means that the binder must be liquid, e. g. in a two-component floor coating.
• Mixed-mode drying, where chemically hardening binders are dissolved in (aqueous or organic) solvents which evaporate in parallel with the hardening reaction. The type of chemical hardening process here varies. In single-component materials, the hardening component may come from the surroundings (oxygen, moisture, carbon dioxide) or from the surface (if it is mineral). An example of mineral hardening is silification (see table 11).

Calcimine
White lime Ca(OH)$_2$ thinned with water is used as the binder.
Pure calcimine is a single-component paint. It hardens onto the wall due to evaporation of the solvent water. The additional reaction with carbon dioxide from the air causes carbonation to calcite and therefore the final hardening. The pigments must be lime-fast, e. g. all mineral pigments. Natural mineral pigments include chalk (whiting), lime (white lime), cement (white cement), ochre (alumina), umbra (alumina) or green earth (weathered hornblende) They are made by mechanical treatment of the raw material – by milling, elutriation, drying or calcining. Synthetic mineral pigments also belong to this group, e. g. titanium white, zinc white or cobalt blue. In order not to decrease the hardening capacity of calcimine, the mixture may contain no more than 10 % pigment by volume.

Calcimine is very maintenance-intensive and is generally used as an exterior paint only on historical buildings as appropriate for the existing building substance. On exterior surfaces there is a danger of the lime fraction turning to gypsum due to reaction with acid rain. Lime whiting with no colour pigments was formerly used to whitewash simple rooms and stalls. Thanks to its high pH value, lime whiting also acts as a disinfectant.
Today, these paints are being rediscovered for interior use because of their moisture equilibrium promoting properties and the brightness of their colours, known as the lime lustre effect. Calcimine is very open to diffusion and absorbs a lot of water but releases it again quickly. The weathering quality can be improved by hydraulic additions or linseed oil.

Cement paints
Cement slurries, watery cement suspensions produced by slurrying with water have been in use for a long time. They have good water and weather resistance and are suitable for use under water or in wet rooms or cold storage rooms.

Distemper, casein paint
Distemper and casein paint are particularly suitable for interior use. They no longer hold a large market share, but are still used in ecologically-friendly construction projects. A size solution – originally made from bones, but today made from vegetable starch – is used as the binder. Almost all pigments with good coverage can be used. Since it is an organic material, size can be a good culture medium for bacteria, and may therefore only be used in dry rooms on a dry surface. If the amount of size in the coating is too low, it will not be wipe resistant. If too much size is present, stress cracking and peeling will result.

Casein is a milk protein. Together with lime, the yellowish powder reduces to form water-soluble size. Casein distemper hardens by drying, and partly by reacting with lime in the surface.

10 Left: Flake of emulsion paint, coalescent
   Centre and right: Flake of silicone resin and
   silicate paint, non-coalescent
11 The hardening process in paints
12 Ceiling painting from the Lascaux caves, about
   15.000 BC.
13 The colour effect of calcimine

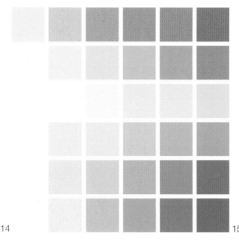

14

15

Silicate paint

Silicate paints, also known as pure silicate, two-component silicate or waterglass paints, are made from a liquid water glass solution, alkali-resistant pigments and fillers with no organic additions. Potassium water glass is silicic sodium or potassium as a syrup-like liquid made by melting quartz sand with potash or soda. It is used as a binder for silicate paints under the patented-protected designation "Fixative". The development of silicate paints began towards the end of the 19th century, at first purely as artists' paints for frescos and facade paintings. Pure silicate paints are supplied as two-component systems consisting of a 20–30% potassium silicate solution, the Fixative and coloured powder (earth and inorganic, mineral pigments and fillers). They must still be mixed by the craftsmen a day before they are required, and left to swell.

After the water solvent has evaporated, the pigments in the silicate paint bond with one another and with the mineral surface containing lime or silicate, by reacting with carbon dioxide in the air (see fig. 16).
As the paint hardens it does not coalesce to a continuous film but rather reacts chemically and petrifies or causes a silification of the mineral surface. The resulting coating is very porous and therefore very permeable by water vapour, mineral, insoluble, flame retardant and incombustible. It is particularly suited to mineral backgrounds which are capable of silification. These include lime, lime-cement and cement plasters/renders, sandy limestone, brick and natural stone. Thanks to its high CO_2-permeability, silicate paint is also suitable for carbonaticbound mortars which require carbon dioxide to harden. The surface must usually be roughed or fluated to remove any sintered layers present in new plaster/rendering or any remaining emulsion paint.

According to DIN 18363, silicate paints are not approved for use with gypsum surfaces. Similarly they are only permissible under certain conditions for use with concrete, since the high CO_2 permeability is deleterious to the corrosion protection of the reinforcement. Due to their alkaline nature and the wholly inorganic ingredients, silicate paints are antibacterial. The capillarity allows a high vapour permeability but also quick drying. The colours are reminiscent of calcimine with their earth coloured matt brightness, but they do not chalk as quickly and absorb fewer pollutants from the air (see fig. 14). For this reason, silicate paints are often used as a substitute for the traditional calcimine paints in the restoration of historic buildings. Even if multiple coats are applied, the water vapour diffusibility decreases only slightly. In addition, the mineral binder has the same thermal expansion coefficient as the surface, meaning that thermal stresses are avoided. The high alkalinity of silicate paints means that sensitive surfaces such as glass, tiles or metal must be protected from paint drips during painting work, since the drips can not usually be removed without staining.

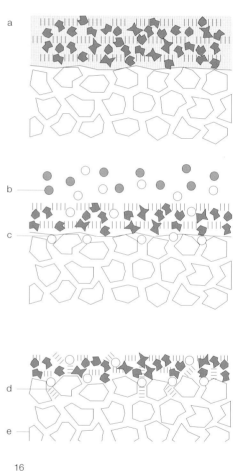

16

14 Colour effect of silicate paints
15 Scanning electron micrograph of the silification zone of a silicate paint coat.
16 Hardening process of silicate paints, chemical hardening
   a Application of the paint
   b Evaporation of water
   c CO_2 is absorbed from the air
   d Bonding with the surface, silification
   e Mineralised surface
17 Colour effect of emulsion-type silicate paints

17

Emulsion-type silicate paint
In contrast to purely silicate paints, emulsion-type silicate paints contain a maximum of 5 % organic binders by volume, in addition to the potassium water glass binder, in the form of a polymer emulsion. This limit is defined in DIN 18363 in order to retain the mineral character of the single-component system. The polymer emulsion used must be compatible with water glass and alkali-resistant. Styrene acrylate dispersions are usually used for this reason.

The pigments must not react uncontrollably with the water glass, so only inorganic pigments and natural, crystalline calcite fillers are used. The available pigments mean that only a limited scale of bright matt colours is possible (see fig. 17). The system dries physically and at the same time adhesively due to the evaporation of water, as well as chemically due to the silification of the water glass binder. Emulsion-type silicate paints bond with all mineral surfaces and combine the advantages of silicate paints – the high vapour permeability – with the low water absorption of emulsion paints.

The low emulsion content does not allow coalescence, but does reduce the absorption of water with no negative effect on the water vapour diffusion.

These coating systems therefore belong to those with the lowest moisture equilibrium and are offered, with the advantage of their easy-to-use, single-component system, by all major manufacturers. Emulsion-type silicate paints can be used on both interior and exterior surfaces. The emulsion addition increases the shelf-life and the adhesion of the paint. Even drying and bonding on older surfaces are improved. Chalking of exterior house paints is reduced. The colours are light-fast and weatherproof. A base coat which enables the hardening process must first be applied to gypsum and organic, older paintwork.

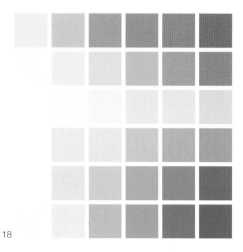

18

Silicone resin emulsion paint
Silicone resin emulsion paints consist of polymer emulsions (usually acrylate dispersions), pigments, fillers, auxiliary substances and silicone resin emulsions. The binder consists of polymer emulsion and silicone emulsion in equal proportions. Water is used as a solvent. After the water has evaporated (physical drying), the silicone resin remains and bonds adhesively with the pigments. Simultaneously, the polymer emulsions react chemically with one another to form a type of silicone resin network (silification). By this process, and in contrast to the sealed film formed by emulsion paints, a microporous film is formed, which allows the paint to remain very permeable to water vapour despite its hydrophobing solution. The pores are not hermetically sealed, but the capillaries are hydrophobically closed. Silicone resin emulsion paints are increasing in popularity because they, like emulsion-type silicate paints, preclude the disadvantages of purely silicate or emulsion systems. Due to the small proportion of polymer emulsion, approx. 5 % by volume, the coating is strongly water-repellent (low w-value) despite its good water vapour diffusion (low sd-value). The combination of the polymer emulsion with a silicone resin emulsion allows a high vapour permeability without increasing the absorption of water, because the silicone resin hydrophobes the pores formed. The objective of these systems is to achieve a water absorption coefficient $w < 0.1$ kg/(m²h$^{0.5}$) and s_d-values < 0.1 m. The emulsion fraction is necessary to reduce chalking and increase the abrasion resistance. Since the ingredients, but not their exact ratios, are laid out in DIN 18363, these should be checked before selection.

The paint is suitable for mineral surfaces and can be used on new or existing plastered/rendered surfaces. It is weatherproof and resistant to air-borne pollutants and dirt. Because it is not thermoplastic and stays dry for long periods of time, the danger of algal or mould growth is reduced. The paint is easy to paint over and behaves favourably in the case of fire. The range of colours is similar to that of the silicate paints (see fig. 18)

Silicone resin paints
Siloxane or silicone resin paints contain siloxane and acrylic resin binders dissolved in organic solvents. Their constitution means that they only evaporate slowly. The difference between these paints and silicone resin emulsion paints lies in the solvent. They are mainly used to hydrophobe surfaces (see p. 72, waterproofing substances).

19

20

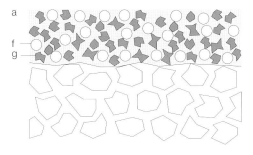

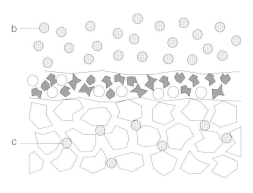

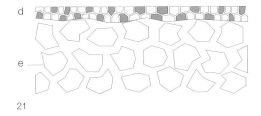

21

18 Colour effect of silicone resin emulsions
19 Scanning electron micrograph of an emulsion
     paint film
20 Colour effect of emulsion paints
21 Hardening process of an emulsion paint, physi-
     cal drying
     a Application of the paint
     b Evaporation of the water
     c Water is absorbed by the surface
     d Coalescence by cold flow, the melting of
         polymer components without the influence of
         heat, at ambient temperature
     e Surface
     f Polymer emulsion
     g Pigments

Polymer dispersion paint
The name of the polymer dispersion paints comes from the binder, a polymerisation resin dispersed in water. Depending on the requirements, plasticisers, fillers and pigments are added. The spherical polymer particles (0.1–3.0 µm) are mainly made from acrylates, styrene acrylates or polyvinyl acetates and are finely dispersed, not dissolved, in the water. This condition is known as a dispersion. The pigments are inorganic, e.g. titanium dioxide or iron oxide and provide a wide range of colours (see fig. 20).

The drying of the paint ends in coalescence (see fig. 21). After the paint has been applied, the solvent water penetrates the surface being coated and presses the polymer spheres into it. This causes the paint to stick to the surface. Simultaneously, water evaporates from the shrinking film, the polymer particles are pressed together and melt into a continuous film. As an organic system, the paint does not bond with the mineral background, but rather glues to its surface. The properties of this film can be influenced by additives, such that sufficient water vapour can escape without affecting the high weathering quality of the paint.

Since their development at the beginning of the last century, emulsion paints have taken a leading position in the market due to their ease of application and multiplicity of uses. As paints, which can be thinned with water and used as a single-component system, the polymer dispersion paints as defined in DIN 55945, which coalesce and therefore have a high strength and weathering resistance, form a transition to the paints which can be thinned by solvents, e.g. oil paints and varnishes. They can be used on mineral, timber or metal surfaces. They are suita-

ble for use on both interior and exterior surfaces. They are wipe and abrasion resistant. The wipe-resistant variety is commonly referred to as latex paint. The diffusibility decreases when multiple layers of paint are applied on top of each other. Since lime mortar, for example, can then no longer be supplied with the CO_2 it requires, old coats of paint should be stripped or burnt off.

Polymerisate resin paints
Polymerisate resin paints are solvent-based emulsion paints. The binder is generally an acrylic resin or vinyl acetate solution. This is combined with siloxanes. These increase the hydrophobing effect and the vapour permeability, although the siloxanes themselves only have a limited permeability to carbon dioxide. Thanks to these properties they are primarily used to coat concrete, but can be used on all other mineral surfaces or paints. They are used in areas with a high degree of atmospheric pollution. Due to the solvent content they cannot be used with plaster/rendering systems which contain polystyrene. They can, however, also be applied during the cold season.

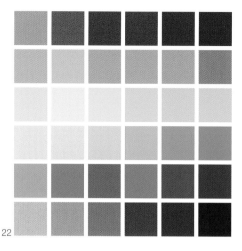

22

Varnishes

A wide range of varnishes are in use. They can generally be divided into two categories: water varnishes, i.e. those that have water as a solvent; and those that contain solvents. Water varnishes, which are not detrimental to health, are available for almost all applications today. In addition, the varnishes can be classified as either single or two-component systems. The following varnishes are described in DIN 18363:
· Polymerisate resin paints (see p. 69)
· Epoxy resin varnishes (EP varnishes)
· Polyurethane varnishes (PUR varnishes)
· Alkyd varnishes
· Cellulose nitrate lacquer
· Acrylic resin varnish
· Acid-hardening, cold-curing paints
· Synthetic resin plasters
· Chlorinate rubber lacquers
· Cyclorubber lacquers
· Multi-effect paints
· Tar pitch combination varnishes
· Radiator paint consisting of heat-resistant alkyd resin combinations
· Silicone resin varnish (see p. 68)
· Bituminous varnish
· Bronzing lacquer

Synthetic resin paints

Today, synthetic resin paint is a term used for alkyd resin paints which contain solvents. From a chemical viewpoint, alkyd resin is a product of carboxylic acid, alcohol and oils and/or fatty acids. The use of pigments and fillers is virtually unlimited. Hardening is achieved chemically, after evaporation of the solvent, white spirit, in the presence of oxygen from the air, but is relatively slow, so that hardening accelerators are added to catalyse the reaction. Alkyd resin paints are used for building construction and decoration purposes on iron, steel and timber surfaces. They are easy to use and apply, very easy to sand (particularly for renovation paintwork) and, as a single-component material, largely environmentally and user-friendly. They should not be used on mineral, alkaline or galvanized surfaces.

Acrylic varnishes

Acrylic is used as a binder in many combinations. Finely dispersed in an aqueous solution, it is known as a plastic or polymer dispersion and forms the basis of house paints, the polymer dispersion paints described above. In contrast to the aqueous acrylates, the binders here are in solution. The solvent evaporates, the individual polymer molecules become entangled, "matting", and harden purely physically. Acrylic paints which contain solvents have very good adhesion properties on a variety of surfaces, have a low vapour diffusibility and are highly impervious to CO_2. They are used on galvanized surfaces, plastics or concrete.

Two-component coating materials

Two-component coating materials (cold-curing resins) generally consist of two components, which are mixed together shortly before the material is to be used. One component is known as the paint, the other as the hardener. After the solvent has evaporated, the film shrinks and the molecules of the binder move closer together. The hardener component reacts chemically with the reactive binders in the paint. Attention must be paid to correct mixing and to the pot life. The resulting coatings are characterised by their high imperviousness to CO_2 and water vapour and their good resistance to solvents and chemicals. They are suitable for use as impervious and hard floor coverings, for crack bridging, corrosion protection and on timber (doors and parquet) and plastic surfaces. There are three types: solid to viscoelastic epoxy resin systems, elastic polyurethane systems, and acid-hardening systems.

22 Colour effect of varnishes
23 Steel section with foamed coating
24 Building material and fire classifications
25 Fire classifications

23

Fireproof paint

Fire-protection measures are designed to protect people's lives and health. To achieve these goals, the combustibility of the building materials and the behaviour of building elements in the case of fire are defined in fire protection ratings (see table 24).
Endangered building elements can be clad with non-combustible materials, e. g. gypsum plasterboard, or protected by a coating.

Steel girders and sections lose their strength above about 500 °C. Timber beams are combustible, but demonstrate advantageous behaviour in fires if they are oversized. In a fire, they first develop an outer layer of charcoal. This protects the undamaged timber from heating further and losing its strength. Ignition can be delayed, and therefore also the spreading of the fire, by an intumescent – swelling – paint. Temperatures above 200 °C cause a chemical reaction in the paint, causing it to foam. The foamed layer is porous and contains a lot of carbon. This means that only a low amount of heat can pass through. The thickness of the normal dry layer is 200–2.000 μm, the foam achieves 40 to 120 times the volume,

equating to a thickness of around 5 cm. The necessary space for the foaming reaction must be taken into account during construction.
The basis of the fireproof paint can be emulsion paints, usually aqueous polymer dispersions, or varnishes, usually acrylic resin varnishes. The specific components are intumescent additions consisting of a carbon source, a catalyst and a foaming agent.

Timber
Timber and wooden materials with a coating are classified as B 1 flame proof rather than B 2 normally flammable, at temperatures up to 900 °C. The systems currently available for the treatment of timber are only approved for interior use. Also, the relative humidity of the wooden materials must not exceed 70–80 %.
A higher humidity can be combated by using an approved top coat in addition to the fireproof paint.
The coating can also take the form of a transparent protective varnish.

Steel
Flame-retardant coatings with a fire classification of F 30 or F 60 can be used on steel girders, pillars and frame members

on the exterior or in interior spaces. One must differentiate between open and closed sections since the necessary thickness of the coating depends on the ratio of circumference to area = C/A. The top coat can be supplied in almost any colour.

The following points must be observed in an invitation to tender:
• Declaration of the fire classification
• For use on the exterior or interior
• Open or closed section
• C/A value required
• Composition of the system, comprising:
  1 Corrosion protection
  2 Intumescent material
  3 Covering coat
• Minimum thickness of the dried layer
• Lining and casing

Table 24   Examples of building materials and their fire classification/European classification

Building material	Material class	European classification acc. to DIN 4102-1
Incombustible building materials (e. g. steel, concrete)	A 1	A 1
Incombustible building material with combustible components (e. g. plasterboard)	A 2	A 2
Flame-proof building material (e. g. oak parquet flooring on cement-and-sand screed)	B 1	B
Small contribution to fire		C
Normally flammable building material (e. g. timber and wooden materials)	B 2	D
Acceptable behaviour in the case of fire		E
Flammable building material (e. g. untreated coir mats)	B 3	F

Table 25

Fire classification	Fire resistant period in min	Construction authority designations
F 30	≥ 30	flame-retardant
F 60	≥ 60	flame-retardant
F 90	≥ 90	fire-resistant
F 120	≥ 120	fire-resistant
F 180	≥ 180	highly fire-resistant

26   27

Impregnating agents
Impregnating agents are low-viscosity capillary-active dispersions or binder solutions. They generally contain neither pigments nor fillers, and dry to a transparent finish. They are used on porous surfaces such as plaster/rendering, concrete, stone, timber, cloth or textiles, but also on smooth surfaces such as gypsum or metals. Depending on the requirements, impregnating agents chemically neutralise the surface to be treated, they are water-repellent (hydrophobic) and seal out greasy or oily substances. They protect against damaging environmental influences, against bacteria, animal and vegetable pests (mould, insects and moss), reduce the water absorption capacity of the surface, strengthen it and act as a bond coat.

Impregnating agents include:
• Base coats
• Sealants
• Primers
• Putty, filler
• Degreasing and cleaning agents
• Anticorrosive agents
• Hydrophobing agents
• Timber preservatives

Base coats
These bind loose particles on the surface of mineral plasters/renders and thus improve the adhesion of the surface. To reduce the water absorption of the material, small pores are closed. This prevents an excessively rapid "wicking away" of the solvent or water – known as firing-on – of the next coat.
Base coats do not coalesce but penetrate deep into the capillaries of the surface. They are also known as deep primers. Polymerisate resins, silanes, silicone resins, silicic-acid ester or water glass are used for this purpose. They can simultaneously serve as a hydrophobing agent.

Hydrophobing agents
Hydrophobing a material or coating can increase its life and maintenance interval. In contrast to paints which form a film or layer on the surface of the plaster/rendering, hydrophobing agents are impregnating agents which do not close the capillaries.

Besides these capillary-active systems there are also silicon resin systems, which, analogous to the surface of a lotus leaf, have a particular surface roughness that causes water drops to pearl off taking particles of dirt with them. In contrast to the surface of the lotus leaf, which is in constant renewal, the application of this coating is a one-off process. Uniform weathering is important for a homogeneous coating. Today, mainly aqueous systems, or systems containing solvents are used, which are based on organic silicon compounds and with silicone resin as the final product. Silanes and siloxanes belong to this group, as do siliconates, which, however, bring with them the danger of salt formation. Traditional hydrophobing agents such as gelatine or size have a limited life. Water glass leads to a graying of the plaster/rendering surface, linseed or poppyseed oil lends the surface a high gloss. Although hydrophobing agents are generally transparent and penetrate the surface, they cause the coating to become darker.

Timber preservative according to DIN 68800
Timber preservatives or impregnating varnishes must penetrate deep into the timber. Industrially the penetration depth is improved using pressure and vacuum equipment – the pressure process. Varnishes which contain solvents are made from alkyd resin with a high oil content and combinations of natural resin and oil, aqueous impregnating agents based on alkyd resins and natural resin oil emulsions or, more rarely, acrylic resin. Aqueous impregnating varnishes do not penetrate the timber so deeply, however, are not as water-repellent and are less easy to sand.

A timber preservative should be selected that carries the RAL mark and is approved by the German Institute for Construction Engineering, which certifies that the impregnating agent and its biocidal, fungicidal and insecticidal components are not detrimental to health. Some older timber preservatives are detrimental to health and are therefore no longer permitted. These include the previously commonly used fungicide PCP (pentachlorophenol) and the insecticide Lindan. Structures which have been treated with these substances are considered contaminated and must be disposed of.

26 Silane-siloxane aqueous hydrophobing base
    coat
27 Pigmented acrylate aqueous hydrophobing base
    coat used to strengthen old paintwork
28 Covering cement coatings
    a   Base coat, coloured or transparent
    b   Top coat with washed concrete protective
        coating, 2
29 Scumble glaze for concrete
    a   Deep primer to prevent the formation of stains
        due to differences in the absorption of water
    b   Concrete scumble glaze, coloured, 2
30 Concrete rehabilitation; expose the corroded
    steel and coat with an approved rust-protection
    system
31 Concrete rehabilitation; brush the exposed areas
    with an adhesive slurry and level using a filler
32 Sanitation of concrete; level the surface with a
    scratch coat and fine filler

28

29

30

31

32

Concrete

Concrete is a mineral substance. Fresh concrete is highly alkaline (pH > 12.5). The alkalinity of the concrete protects its reinforcement from corrosion. If the alkalinity is lowered by carbon dioxide (CO_2) or other acidic compounds in the air, the steel begins to corrode at a pH reduced to below 9.5 by moisture and oxygen. A minimum lapping of 3, or even better, 4 cm should be ensured, or the reinforcing steel will rust. Sufficient lapping is particularly important for ornamental or exposed concrete. Two main uses of coatings on concrete are given here: Coatings as protection against moisture or for aesthetic reasons and coatings as concrete maintenance systems and as corrosion protection of the reinforcement.

Concrete protection

Besides alkali-resistance, the following minimum requirements are valid for protective coatings on concrete surfaces:
- The resistance to diffusion of carbon dioxide: the equivalent air layer thickness, sd (CO_2), must be > 50.0 m.
- The resistance to the diffusion of water vapour: the equivalent air layer thickness, sd (H_2O), must be < 4.0 m.
- Crack-bridging to a width of 0.15 mm must be possible.

The surface must be solid, free of friable particles and weakly absorbent There must be no residual formwork lubricant present, no sintered layer or cement slurries on the surface. Cavities and coarser pores must be closed. The coating system consists of a pigmented or colourless base coat, which is applied to the surface as a bonding agent, strengthener or hydrophobing agent, e.g. dissolved polymer resins; polymer dispersion paints; epoxy, polyurethane, or acrylic resin; silanes or siloxane solutions. The intermediate and finish coats are based on polymer emulsions, dissolved polymer resins or cold-curing resins.

Concrete maintenance

Corroded reinforcing steel must be exposed, blasted – usually to a surface finish according to DIN of SA 2 – have the rust removed and be coated with a corrosion protection agent, such as a plastic-modified cement slurry or a cold-curing system such as epoxy resin. The open areas are then filled with a filling compound, e.g. cement mortar or concrete, with a polymer addition (PCC, polymer cement concrete) or cold-curing mortar (PC, polymer concrete) where necessary. Before applying the intermediate and finish coat the surface is levelled using a fine filler. This can be a plastic-modified cement-bound, cement-modified dispersion-bound or cold-curing resin material.

33

34

Exterior rendering

Exterior rendering must be protected from rising damp and from moisture penetrating through the back of the wall by the use of drainage inclines, drip heads and coverings. The paint chosen must be suitable for the rendering base in question. To achieve a safe and long-lasting facade protection system, the following physical criteria must be considered in addition to the compatibility of the binders: The water absorption coefficient of the coating, the vapour permeability, and the material strength must decrease from the inner to the outer layer. This means that in accordance with Künzel's facade protection theory, the outer coating must meet the following classifications:
$w < 0.5 \ kg/m^2h^{0,5}$, $sd < 2.0 \ m$ and
$w \cdot sd < 0.1 \ kg/mh^{0,5}$.
This ensures a low moisture equilibrium.

Every plastering/rendering mortar group requires a particular coating material (see Appendix, table: Coatings on Plaster/Rendering, p. 103). Accordingly, polymer dispersion paints may not be used on lime plasters, mortar group P I a/b, because they do not allow the passage of sufficient carbon dioxide to carbonatize the plaster. Purely silicate paints, on the other hand, may not be used on rendering which contains gypsum, MG P IV b/d, since in this case silification cannot occur without the use of additional admixtures. Rendering that contains lime or cement always reacts in an alkaline manner with moisture. The chosen coating materials must therefore be alkali-resistant.

The coating system consists of a primer, one or more intermediate coats and a finish coat. The primer promotes bonding and adhesion. Sintered surfaces or old layers of paint must be, for example, fluated to promote silification of silicate paints. Old paintwork can also be burnt off, depending on the binder used.
A base coat may also be used to strengthen the surface or to reduce the absorption capacity of the material. A hydrophobing or impregnating agent with a fungicidal or biocidal function may be used as a final coat on top of the top coat (see p. 72).

The following paints are generally used today on mineral rendering:
• Calcimine
• Silicate paints
• Emulsion-type silicate paints
• Silicone resin emulsion paints
• Emulsion paints and varnishes
• Polymerisate paints

In addition there are synthetic resin plasters and textured coatings, which are essentially paints with the appearance of plaster, based on silicates, silicone resin emulsions or synthetic resin-modified lime cement. These are primarily used as a thin top coat on external thermal insulation composite systems.

The rendering base must be checked before the coating is applied (see Appendix, p. 104). The rendering must be even and not friable. As a rule of thumb, the coating can be applied after a drying time of approximately four weeks, depending on the thickness of the rendering and on the weather conditions. The rendering must be strong when dry and wetted, absorbent and wettable, free of dust and loose or friable particles, and free from sintering and blooming. The reinforcement or rendering base must not be exposed or be visible on the surface. The surface must be free of cracks. Shrinkage cracks of up to 0.1 mm in a smooth, fine surface and up to 0.2 mm in a surface with a grain size of 3 mm are to be discounted.

Plaster/rendering can be directly coloured using pigments. However, the coloured rendering mortar can dry to give a mottled appearance depending on the weather conditions. Even the correct application of the rendering cannot prevent this characteristic appearance. This is not a structural defect, however. The surface, which can be deemed uneven or decorative depending on your viewpoint, can be evenly coloured by applying an equalisation coat. This single coat is listed separately in the bill of quantities.

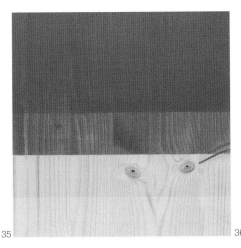

35 36 37

Coatings on timber

Coatings are used on timber to protect the anisotropic material against moisture, cracking due to swelling and shrinking, temperature changes, mould, insect attack, discolouring due to pigments (resins) in the wood itself and UV light (preventing blueing). They provide mechanical protection and also serve a decorative purpose. Timber used on exterior surfaces, which is more heavily loaded than timber used in interior spaces, is divided into two groups: dimensionally stable timber elements and timber elements that are dimensionally unstable or of limited dimensional stability. Windows and doors are considered dimensionally stable, whereas facade cladding, timber frames, roof soffits and fences or pergolas are considered dimensionally unstable.
The timbers, which are classified according to their resistivity (see also Detail Practice Timber Construction), may only contain residual moisture before coating. The moisture content, measured at multiple locations at a depth of 5 mm, must not exceed 15 % for softwoods and 12 % for hardwoods. They must always be treated with an impregnating varnish or chemical timber protection agent (see p. 72).

Both covering and scumbling coatings can be used for timber. Covering coatings are achieved using emulsion paints and emulsion lacquers as a pigmented, water-thinned coating material or as pigmented, solvent-thinned lacquers, generally with an alkyd resin base.

Scumble glazes are coating materials with special scumble pigments, which result in a coloured but transparent coating. The final colour effect is determined by the colour of the scumble glaze, but also by the intrinsic colour of the timber itself. Thick-coating scumble glazes and thin-coating scumble glazes are used for different purposes.

The binders used in thick-coating scumble glazes are either high-viscosity alkyd resins containing solvents, or acrylic and/or alkyd resin binders that can be thinned using water. They are used, with a blueing protection agent, as intermediate and final coats and for maintenance purposes on dimensionally stable building elements. Since moisture can often enter dimensionally unstable building elements such as facade linings via the construction joints, the coating used must allow moisture equalisation. Thin-coating scumble glazes, also known as impregnating varnishes, are generally used for this purpose as a base, intermediate and top coat. They contain either alkyd resin solvent binders or acrylic and/or alkyd resin binders which can be thinned with water. On timbers which are susceptible to mould, the scumble glazes can contain a suitable fungicide. For dimensionally stable building elements, thin coating scumble glazes are generally only used as a base coat. Scumble glazes should be checked approximately every two years, covering coatings every four years.

33 Coatings on rendered concrete, e.g.
   a Colourless deep primer
   b Base coat as a bond coat with a quartz content
   c Rubbed-finish rendering, grain size 1.5 mm
   d Covering silicone resin paint, 2
34 Coating on old paintwork, e.g.
   a Removal of the sintered layer by fluating.
   b Application of the base coat with a crack-bridging silicate slurry addition
   c Covering coating with silicate paint, 2
35 Thick-coating timber scumble glaze
   a Impregnating against blueing
   b Acrylic-based polymer dispersion varnish, 2
36 Thin-coating timber scumble glaze
   a Impregnating against blueing
   b Alkyd resin scumble glaze containing solvents, 2
37 Wood lacquer
   a Impregnating against blueing (in softwoods)
   b Insulating timber base coat to seal in the coloured pigments in the wood
   c Intermediate coat with a coloured enamel undercoat
   d Finish covering coat

38

Coatings on glass
Glass can be coloured by different methods. The glass can either be coloured throughout its thickness during the melting or casting processes, or coloured using a liquid or powder sputter coating, or screen printed or enamelled, or a film can be glued to its surface.
Coloured coatings are primarily used for facade cladding and interior decoration. Transparent coatings, some with metal oxides, are used as protection against the sun and as insulation on glass facades.

Organic lacquers
Lacquers used for glass are generally acrylate based and contain solvents. Alternatively, aqueous polyurethane lacquers can be used. The lacquers can be used for scumbling or covering. They are also used by glaziers as a clear lacquer to produce a matt effect. A complete range of colour systems is available. The lacquers are applied manually using rollers or by spraying, or industrially by passing the cast glass under a "curtain" of lacquer. The surface must be cleaned and degreased and usually treated with a bonding agent, which can be contained in the lacquer itself. The lacquers must possess sufficient resistance to scratching and be UV-fast as well as resistant to cleaning substances.

Melting process
Coloured glass is produced by adding pigments during the melting process used to produce float glass, the most common glass building material today. The machine-drawn flat glass is coloured through its entire thickness and is supplied as safety glass or prestressed. Smaller quantities of coloured float glass can also be supplied.
The colour of the glass is produced by the absorption of light of certain wavelengths. Normal float glass appears to be green. This colour is principally due to iron oxides. By adding, for example, cobalt, iron or chrome, yellow, green, blue and red colours and tints or greys can be produced. The glass sheets can be manufactured in dimensions up to 2100 x 1500 mm.

The fusing process can be used to melt different coloured glasses together. Clear load-bearing glass can also be coated during production. This results in a milk flashed glass, a white-coloured, translucent glass used for light-diffusing ceilings.

Table 39

Colouring agent	Glass colour	
Copper	Cu^{2+}	pale blue
Chrome	Cr^{3+}	green
Chrome	Cr^{6+}	yellow
Manganese	Mn^{3+}	violet
Iron	Fe^{3+}	yellow-brown
Iron	Fe^{2+}	blue-green
Cobalt	Co^{2+}	bright blue
Cobalt	Co^{3+}	green
Nickel	Ni^{2+}	grey-brown, yellow, green, blue to violet, depending on the matrix of the glass
Vanadium	V^{3+}	green, brown
Titanium	Ti^{3+}	violet
Neodymium	Nd^{3+}	red-violet
Praseodymium	Pr^{3+}	pale green

Coatings on metals

The requirements of the coloured coatings differ. They depend on the corrosion behaviour of the individual metals.

Iron, steel

Iron and steel are made from naturally-occurring iron oxides – a process which requires large amounts of energy. During oxidation, accelerated by the presence of salt and moisture, the materials tend towards the low-energy state again, corrosion or "rust" occurs. Steel and iron constructions must therefore be protected from corrosion (see Appendix, table: Corrosion Protection, p. 107) and this can only be achieved by using paints. A zinc dust coating, the fabrication primer, is usually used as the base coat. It protects the metal during transport and storage. Before applying the intermediate or top coat, the surface must be washed with a netting agent and wet ground, depending on the type of surface. Almost all solvent and water-based lacquers and emulsions can be applied to this prepared surface.

Top coats protect the actual rust-protection coating from water, salt and chemicals, and keep oxygen from penetrating to the underlying surface. Micaceous fillers in particular increase the diffusion path for any moisture entering the system, and so form an effective barrier, also against mechanical stresses.

Zinc, galvanized steel

Zinc is used in the form of zinc sheet or as a corrosion-protection coating on steel. The positions of the metals in the electrochemical series mean that the steel is protected by the more reactive zinc. As it corrodes, zinc forms a top coat, which provides some limited protection. This layer is metallic silver to dull grey in colour. Depending on the background, zinc "flowers" may be visible. Components are covered in molten zinc in the hot-dip galvanizing process, where they are dipped in a bath of hot zinc (over 600 °C). An 80–120 µm thick layer is sufficient to protect the component from weathering. The zinc surface can be coated in order to increase the maintenance interval or for decorative reasons. To do this, the surface is wet ground using an ammonia netting agent and may be blasted using a non-metallic blasting material (sweeping). Almost all solvent and water soluble varnishes and emulsion paints can be used as a top coat, apart from alkyd resin-based universal primers. The combination of hot-dip galvanizing and organic coating is known as a duplex system.

Aluminium

Facade sections and sheets, windows and doors are often made from aluminium due to its specific weight, durability and corrosion-resistance. Aluminium, including pure aluminium and all alloys, has a thin but impervious oxide layer on its surface in the natural state. This thin layer lends good protection under normal atmospheric conditions. If this natural layer is mechanically damaged, it heals itself immediately. An additional protecting layer can be added by artificially thickening the oxide layer by means of anodic oxidation in a process known as anodising. This produces metallic colours ranging from the natural silvery colour of the metal to almost black shades of bronze.

Bare, anodised aluminium can be used without the need for further coatings. If a maintenance or decorative coating is required, the surface must be first cleaned, degreased, dried and ground if necessary. Acrylic, polymerisate or alkyd resin based thin-film, single-component bond coats, which react with metal, or two-component epoxy resin coatings are used as a primer. The intermediate and finish coats must be suitable for use with the primer and for the expected operational demands on the component. For normal interior and exterior components, alkyd resin or polymerisate resin lacquers are used. If moisture must be dealt with, epoxy resin lacquers are used. Polyurethane lacquers are used for coatings that are particularly resistant to weathering and chemical attack. The coatings are applied in the factory by spraying or painting with liquid lacquers, or by powder coating and baking.

38 Megaplex Cinema, Vienna, 2001,
    Architect: Rüdiger Lainer Colour
    design: Oskar Putz
39 Colouring agents and glass colour
40 Coating system on steel
    a Sand blasting of the corroded surface
       to a finish of Sa 2¹/²
    b Rust-protection base coat, two coats
    c Rust-protection paint as an intermediate and
       top coat
41 Coating system on zinc sheeting/
    galvanized steel
    a Wash with wetting agent, degreasing and
       removal of the chromate coat with ammonia
       and by wet grinding
    b Adhesion primer for zinc, white
    c Coloured base coat as an intermediate coat
    d Acrylic polyurethane top coat

42

43

44

Corrosion protection

Metallic building materials, especially steel and iron constructions, must be protected from corrosion. This can be achieved by applying phosphate, silicate, cement or metallic coatings (galvanizing) or by painting. The safest option is a duplex system – a combination of metallic coating, galvanizing, and painting (see p. 77).

The construction and thickness of the layers is specified according to the regional location of the site and its atmosphere (e. g. seawater, industry), (see Appendix, Corrosion Protection, p. 107). The surface must be blasted and free of scale, rust and/or old paintwork, according to DIN 12944, with a surface finish of Sa 3 or Sa $2\frac{1}{2}$. For optimal adhesion, a surface roughness of 40 – < 80 µm is specified.

Base coats consist of active pigments which chemically prevent or retard corrosion. The most common of these are zinc and calcium phosphates, zinc white, and metallic zinc dust. These form the base for a zinc-dust paint, commonly but incorrectly known as cold galvanizing.
A normal base coat needs to be 60 µm thick. If the grey or tinted zinc-dust paint is 80–120 µm thick, no top coat is necessary. Each of the coloured intermediate or top coats should also be 60 µm thick, resulting in a total thickness of up to 320 µm and protecting the actual rust-protection coating from damage.

Colour matching

Despite the different ingredients of the paints and coatings, their perceived colours can be compared. Different systems have been developed for this purpose.

The RAL colour system

The RAL colour system, published by the DIN Committee for Delivery Terms and Quality Control (RAL), is widely used and contains 160 common shades in its basic „classic" register. This system is primarily used for paints. The hue (H), chroma (C) and lightness (L) of each colour is defined by number and name (e. g. RAL 3004, purple red). The designation of purple red can be, for example: RAL 3004; H:C:L = 7:2:4. The hue is divided into 24 different shades, the chroma defines the degree of colour saturation in seven graduations and the lightness describes how light or dark the colour is – in up to eight graduations depending on the grey shade. In addition, the sheen can be described, e. g. high gloss or matt.

NCS colours

Alongside the RAL system, the more extensive Scandinavian Natural Colour System, NCS, has established itself for rendering and house paints. The basis is formed by six elementary colours – black, white, blue, red, yellow, green. The NCS colour space is a 3 dimensional double cone in which the exact colour can be located between white and black and the pure colours on its equator.

CIE Lab System

Colour systems based on the CIE system are even more spatial in nature. They are based on organoleptic measurements which are transferred to mathematical models. These serve to exactly define the colour in a diagram, which projects the three-dimensional colour space onto a single surface. The CIE-lab system model used today is based on the four basic colours red, green, blue and yellow.

Samples

In design applications, Pantone colour cards are used, and RGB and CYMK colours are used in printing. Every paint manufacturer, however, issues its own colour cards, meaning that test patches and the comparison of colour samples on site are unavoidable. This is also expressly recommended in the technical guidelines for painters and decorators.

42 Corroded steel section
43 Documentation of the historical paint layers in the courtyard of the Ulmer Hof, in Eichstätt, Germany, 1978–1980. Architect: Karljosef Schattner
44 The paint mixture archive of a plaster / rendering manufacturer

Case studies

Examples of plastering and rendering in use

Mauthausen Visitors' Centre

Floor plan   Scale 1:1500
Vertical section, parapet
Scale 1:20

MSP-H Architekten, Vienna

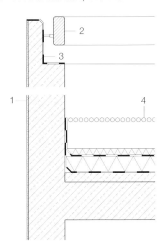

A new visitors' centre has been built for
the former concentration camp at Mau-
thausen. The buildings of the visitors'
centre are clustered close to the original
buildings. To retain the original appearance of the concentration camp, the
entrance level of the new centre has been
kept lower than that of the existing buildings. The space has been allocated to
include an exhibition area, seminar
rooms, a library, archive, shop and office
space. The facades are made from ornamental concrete, natural-coloured
smoothed concrete or glass, depending
on the function of the building.

1   Wall construction:
     6 mm, natural-coloured smoothed concrete;
     200 mm, reinforced concrete
2   60 mm, balustrade dressed larch wood,
     impregnated by heat treatment
3   Sealing layer plastic coating,
     80 mm, reinforced concrete;
     6 mm, natural-coloured smoothed concrete
4   Roof construction, terrace:
     160 mm, gravel granite chippings;
     40 mm, thermal insulation polystyrene;
     roof seal two layers of bitumen sheet;
     80 mm, thermal insulation polystyrene;
     roof seal bitumen sheet;
     60 mm, vapour barrier concrete slope;
     200 mm, reinforced concrete ceiling;
     soffit smoothed

Apartment building in Venice

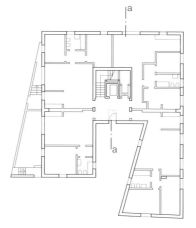

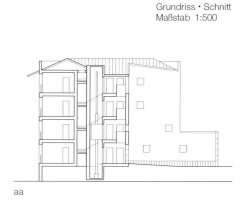

Cino Zucchi architetti, Milan

On the island of Giudecca, near Venice, a former industrial site is being redeveloped as a new residential area. 470 apartments and 300 student apartments have been created on the 32.000 sq. m site since 1997. House "D" is situated at the intersection of two canals, on the northern boundary of the site. The proportions of the building and the materials used are reminiscent of traditional typologies; however some basic features have been newly interpreted, creating an abstract version of the historical archetypes. The facade design makes use of three different window formats: wide and narrow casement doors for living rooms and bedrooms, and square openings for kitchens and bathrooms. The offset pattern of the windows is a result of the different floor plans of the apartments. The window surrounds are created, in the same way as for traditional buildings, using a light-coloured Trani stone, which is similar to the characteristic Istrian limestone of Venice. The proportions of the window surrounds have been changed, however, and have become graphic elements, whose different sizes emphasise the different reveal depths. The plinth of the building is clad using natural stone sheets of different heights. The roof parapet, with the narrow band of natural stone at its upper edge, covers the flat gabled roof on the canal side. Only one part of the surface of the roof is visible. The cubic building has a trapeze-shaped courtyard. The white rendered walls of the courtyard contain marble pigments and stand in stark contrast to the grey rendering of the canal facades. These brick walls are covered in lime rendering containing grey pigments. The rendered walls were not painted, so the surface has a cloudy appearance.

⊔ DETAIL 1/2 2002

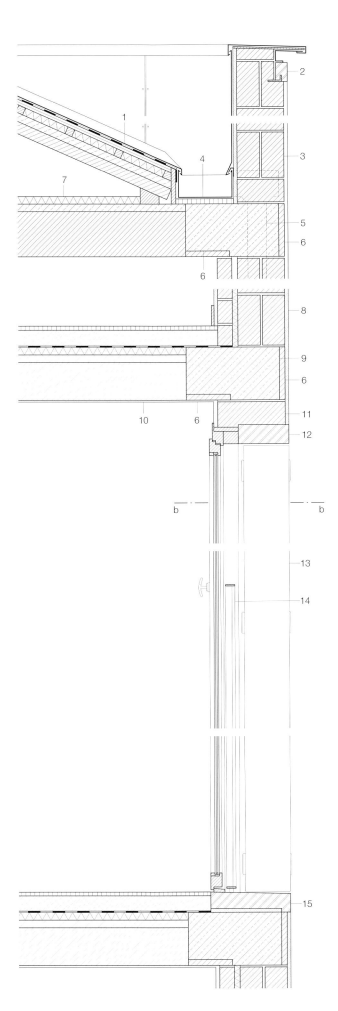

Vertical section · horizontal section   scale 1:20

1 Roof construction
   0.8 mm copper sheet
   bitumen sheet
   25 mm formwork
   40/40 mm bearers
   40 mm thermal insulation, polyurethane
   40 mm reinforced concrete
   60 mm tiled roof elements
   as permanent formwork
2 60/100 mm trani limestone
3 Honeycomb brick
4 Copper rainwater gutter
5 Ø 100 mm roof drainage, PVC pipe
6 30 mm square tiles as a plaster base
7 40 mm expanded clay thermal insulation
8 Wall construction:
   20 mm lime plaster with grey pigments
   250 mm solid brick brickwork
   30 mm thermal insulation, polyurethane
   80 mm honeycomb brick brickwork
   15 mm interior plasterwork
9 Ring beam, reinforced concrete
10 Ceiling Brick elements reinforced
   with concrete topping
11 Brick lintel
12 Lintel, 1100/100/270 mm Trani limestone
13 Folding shutters, ship plywood painted blue-grey
14 Balustrades:
   ⊡ 15/15 mm galvanized steel rods
   in the frame: ⊡ 5/50 mm galvanized steel sheet
15 1100/100/420 mm threshold Trani limestone
16 40 mm cladding Trani limestone

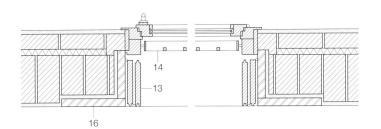

Residential complex in Bonn

Uwe Schröder, Bonn

The residential complex in Bonn consists of 40 two-storey detached houses, built in four rows of five units each, which are grouped around a courtyard. The apartments are designed to meet the needs of a family structure, which is continuously changing. The size and layout of the rooms are designed to be flexible with regard to their use. The sanitary and service areas are in located in the central zones, which do not receive as much light. Plastered concrete balconies and columns frame the open spaces and join the rows to form a cubic unit. The vertical columns and walls of the frame construction are built on individual foundations. The houses stand separately on foundation slabs.

An ochre-grey coloured lime-cement mixture was used for the rendering as both base coat and finish coat. The surface was felted and – due to the smooth 0.5 mm grain size – a mesh was laid into the surface to bridge cracks.

The two post and beam constructions on the front facades are set flexibly into the framework of the building and are joined to each other via the wooden joist ceiling of the ground floor.

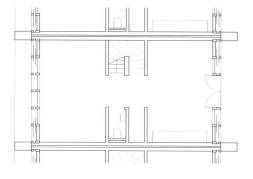

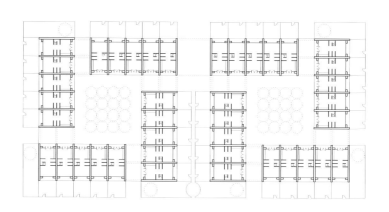

Ground floor, floor plan   Scale 1:200
Site plan   Scale 1:1250

Vertical cross-section
Horizontal cross-section
Scale 1:20

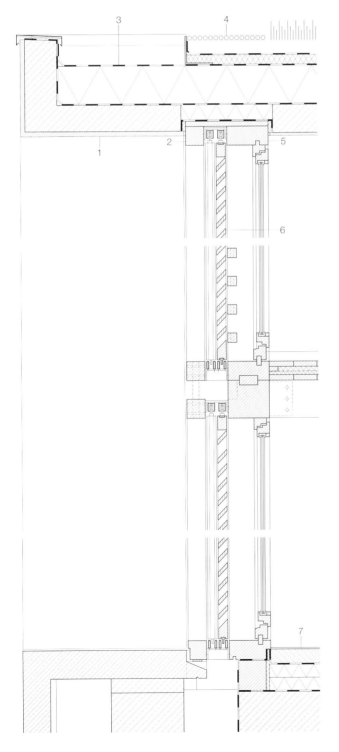

1 Plaster system:
   finish coat, 5 mm lime-cement rendering felted,
   0.5 mm grade
   with a laid-in glass fibre reinforcing mesh
   base coat, 15–20 mm lime-cement plaster
2 100/100 mm timber edge
3 Roof construction:
   sealing layer, bitumen sheet
   thermal insulation,
   210 mm polystyrene rigid foam sheet
   vapour barrier
   hollow section ceiling, 150 mm reinforced concrete
4 Planting of the roof:
   100 mm extensive planting
   filter mat
   drainage layer, 50 mm rigid foam sheeting
   protective and reservoir mat,
   rot-resistant synthetic fibres
   root protection PE sheet
5 100/225 mm timber edge
6 Slatted sliding shutters, larch
7 Floor construction:
   flooring, linoleum
   scree, 75 mm
   polythene sheet separating layer
   thermal insulation, 150 mm polystyrene
   sealing layer, 225 mm reinforced concrete ceiling
8 Interior plasterwork, gypsum plaster,
   15 mm reinforcing mesh
   170 mm brickwork, sandy limestone
9 Plaster system:
   finish coat, 5 mm lime-cement rendering, felted
   0.5 mm grade
   with a laid-in glass fibre reinforcing mesh,
   base coat, 15–20 mm lime-cement plaster
   columns, 400 mm reinforced concrete

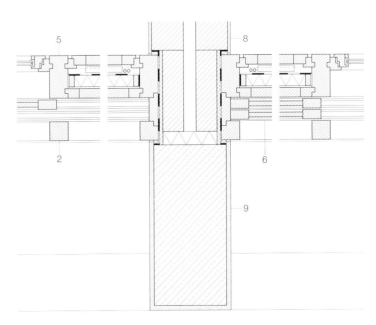

**Catholic Academy
in Stuttgart-Hohenheim**

Arno Lederer, Jórunn Ragnarsdóttir,
Marc Oei, Stuttgart/Karlsruhe

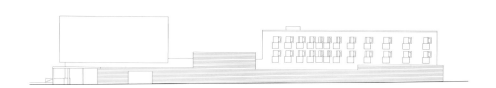

The only site available for the extension of the academy, with 24 rooms, conference rooms and a chapel, was a limited and awkwardly shaped piece of land. The requirement, that all guest rooms face the trees in the park opposite, could not therefore be fulfilled by a linear building, hence the S shaped layout. A new wall of recycled brick joins the older building to the new extension and creates an inward-facing courtyard. Seating niches in the corridor of the ground floor invite you to enjoy the open space devoted to tranquillity and reflection. They occupy the full depth of the curved exterior wall. The glass windows protrude from the plaster-work and, with their wooden mounts, give the impression of picture frames. The surface of the mineral thermal insulation composite system has been textured using a 25 mm thick finish coat of thrown-on trowel plaster. The large grain size, 8 mm, gives the facade a lively texture. The appearance of the extension is dominated by the basket-like balconies of the guest rooms, which correspond in shape with the curved facade. Steel rods have been affixed to the protruding prefabricated concrete slabs, and these rods support a removable wickerwork balustrade.   📖 DETAIL 11/2002

Elevation: north-east
Floor plans
Scale 1:750

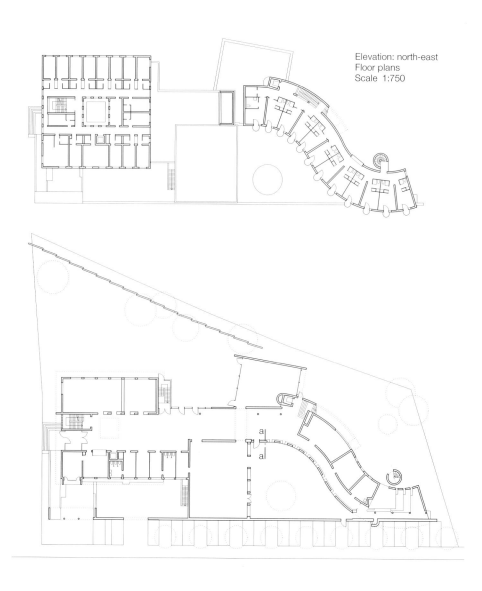

Horizontal section · Vertical section
Seating niches on the ground floor
Scale 1:20

1   240 mm sandy limestone
2   85/264 mm wooden frames, oak
    with insulated double glazing
3   Sealing sheet, EPDM
4   115 mm frost-resistant masonry, brick
5   15 mm interior plasterwork
6   Equalisation coat
    external thermal insulation composite system:
    25 mm, lime-cement rendering, thrown-on
    8 mm grain size
    with reinforcing mesh
    80 mm thermal insulation, mineral wool
    240 mm reinforced concrete wall with glazed finish
    leveling coat lime cement
7   85/264 mm wooden frames, oak
    with insulated double glazing
8   45/500 mm wooden board, painted black

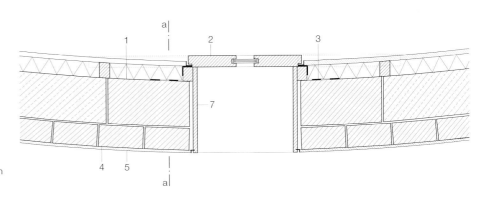

bb

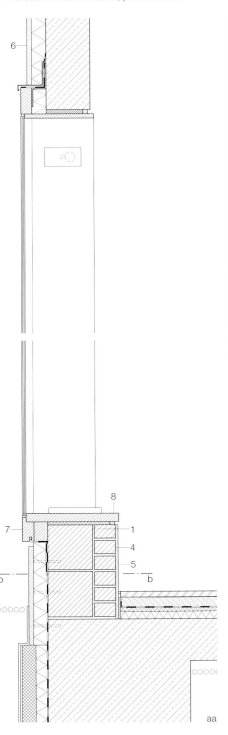

aa

Residential complex Biesdorf-Süd

Léon Wohlhage Wernik Architekten, Berlin

70 residential units in a total of 64 buildings have been constructed in this residential complex in the east of Berlin. The two and three storey terraces form an ensemble of different terraced houses. The floor plans of the individual houses are designed to be so flexible that they can be extended by adding mezzanine floors.
There are some additional entrances, each positioned between two houses, which lead to separate self-contained apartments in the upper storeys and divide up the terraced rows.

The typological diversity of the individual houses is optically brought together by the homogeneous facade design and construction details.
All exterior walls are clad with a mineral thermal insulation composite system, which is coated with yellow-coloured silicate plaster. As a finish, two different red-orange scumble glazes have been added, one applied with a wide brush and the other with a brush-like comb. This technique produced the varied, ingrained appearance of the facade's surface.

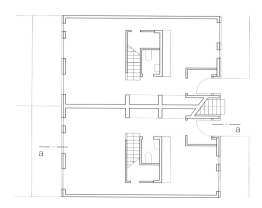

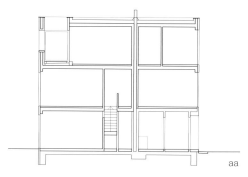

Ground floor, floor plan · Section
Scale 1:250

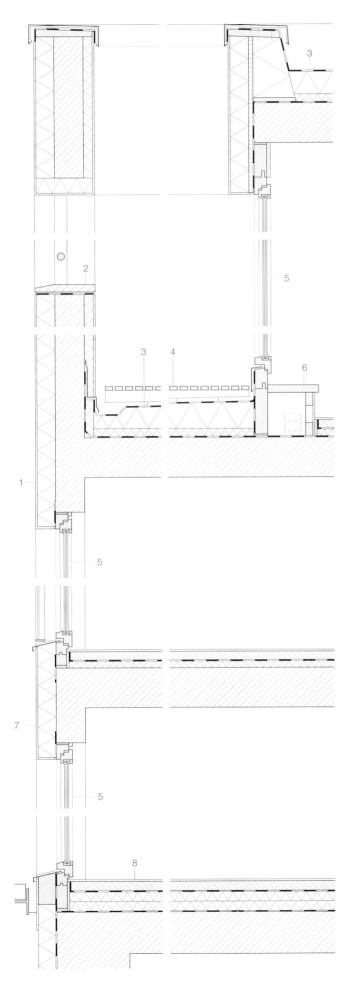

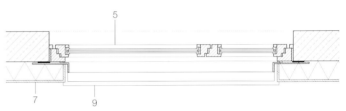

Vertical cross-section
Horizontal cross-section
Scale   1:20

1   wall construction:
    External thermal insulation composite system:
    Red-orange silicate scumble
    top coat 8 mm lightweight plaster, felted,
    grade 1 mm, pigmented yellow and
    with laid-in reinforcing mesh
    100 mm mineral fibre thermal insulation
    160 mm reinforced concrete
2   40 mm pigmented cast stone
3   Roof construction:
    Roof sealing layer: bitumen sheet
    thermal insulation: 150 mm–120 mm polystyrene
    rigid foam sheet on the slope
    thermal insulation:
    40 mm polystyrene rigid foam sheet
    vapour barrier on bitumen primer
    210 mm reinforced concrete ceiling,
    smoothed, painted
4   Lath grating, dressed larch on timber battens
5   Casement door, varnished pine,
    with insulated double glazing
6   230/40 mm tread, maple
    on battens
7   wall construction:
    External thermal insulation composite system:
    Red-orange silicate scumble
    top coat 8 mm lightweight plaster, felted,
    grade 1 mm, pigmented yellow and
    with laid-in reinforcing mesh
    100 mm mineral fibre thermal insulation
    160 mm reinforced concrete
8   Floor construction:
    10 mm carpet
    50 mm scree
    separation layer, PE sheet
    thermal insulation,
    100 mm polystyrene rigid foam sheet
    PE sheet
    foundation plate, 220 mm reinforced concrete
9   Railing frame, 50/10 mm galvanised steel sheet,
    painted with micaceous iron oxide paint

Residential complex in Ljubljana

Bevk Perovic' Architects, Ljubljana

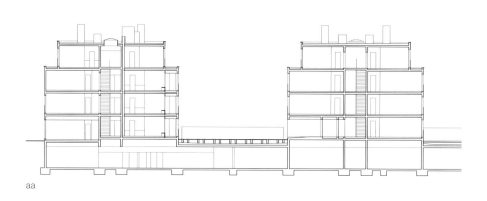

aa

The buildings and facades of this residential complex with 43 apartments in Ljubljana, Slovenia, have been arranged at strict right angles. The graphical arrangement of the windows, doors and balconies, their different sizes and depths and the variations in this pattern and rhythm, break up the strict geometry of the facade. All the openings in the two apartment buildings are framed with steel sections. Like a shadow edge, the metal emphasises the relief-like effect of the exterior wall and simultaneously protects the rendering at the critical corners. The colours of the building emphasise the three dimensional effect of the facade. The muted grey of the facade stands in stark contrast to the yellow walls of the balconies and entrances. The set-back roof storey is a pale sand colour and therefore also optically offset from the other storeys.
The pigmented lime cement rendering top coat was applied as a 20 mm thick scraped finish layer with micaceous feldspar, and emphasises the angular, cubic appearance of the building.

📖 DETAIL 11/2002

Section · Floor plan
Scale 1:500

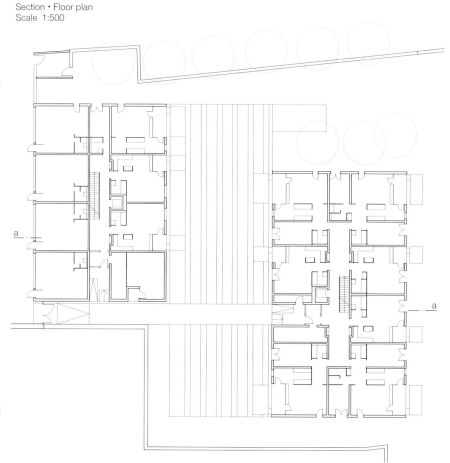

Vertical cross-section   Scale 1:20

1   300/300/20 mm terrazzo tiles
    7 mm thin bed mortar
    48–68 mm screed
    PE sheet
    5 mm bitumen sheet
    30 mm thermal insulation
    170 mm reinforced concrete
2   200/100/4 mm steel section painted
    with drip head
3   External thermal insulation composite system
    20 mm lime-cement plaster scraped finish
    coloured with micaceous feldspar
    80 mm thermal insulation, polystyrene
4   200/100/4 mm steel section painted
5   Textile sunscreen
6   20 mm veneered plywood
7   Balustrade, ⊏⊐ 8 mm sheet steel
8   Sunscreen rail
    25/20 mm aluminium section

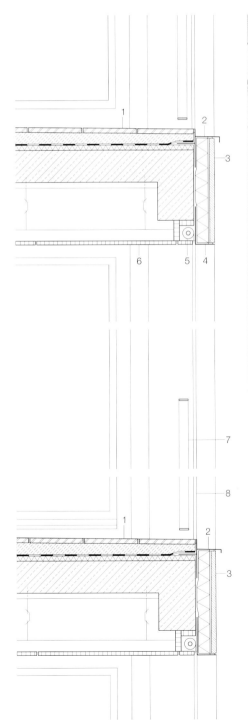

Residential and business premises in Zurich

Marcel Meili,
Markus Peter Architekten, Zurich
Staufen & Hasler Architekten, Frauenfeld

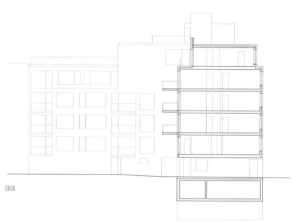

aa

Section · Floor plans
Scale 1:500

This new building in the centre of Zurich, to the south of the main railway station, combines urban living quality with cultural facilities: there are 14 generously proportioned apartments above the cafe and the two-screen cinema.

The cubage of the building and the facade appear simple at first glance, but demonstrate a more subtle design when examined more closely. The design of the facade corresponds to the rendered facades of the neighbouring houses, but the colour has been newly interpreted. Only on closer examination is the pattern of overlapping areas, in lighter and darker colours, apparent. It picks up on the different heights of the windows and, similar to a woven structure, lends depth to the facade. The surface is manifold, in a literal sense: First the deep yellow or red coloured final rendering of the thermal insulation composite system was brushed horizontally or vertically in patches. The grey scumble, subsequently applied, tones down the intensive colours and makes the facade more homogeneous, while allowing the original colours to shine through. The brush strokes give the facade a light texture and the illusion of depth. 　　　　ᒍ DETAIL 12/2003

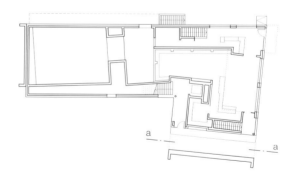

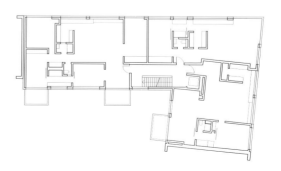

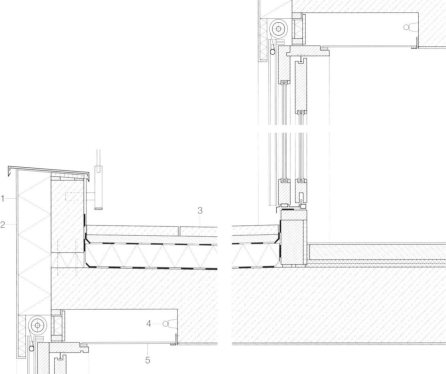

Vertical cross-section
Scale 1:20

1   5 mm rendering construction:
    silicone resin coloured scumble, thinned, grey
    NCS colour s 4502 y, applied with a roller
    final rendering, 1.5 mm grain size, mineral,
    plastic-modified, coloured red and yellow in
    patches, brushed horizontally or vertically
    glass fibre mesh in reinforcing mortar
2   Thermal insulation,
    polystyrene rigid foam sheet
3   Roof construction, inverted roof:
    700/500/40 mm cement panel;
    3/6 mm pigmented chippings, 50 mm
    separating layer, plastic sheet open to diffusion
    thermal insulation, 120 mm extruded polystyrene
    rigid foam sheet
    sealing layer, two layers of bitumen sheet
    430–400 mm reinforced concrete ceiling, sloping
    10 mm gypsum plaster, painted white
4   Fluorescent lighting
5   6 mm white opal acrylic, on an 60/30/50/2 mm
    aluminium angle plate, colourlessly anodised

Parish Community Centre in Munich

Allmann Sattler Wappner, Munich

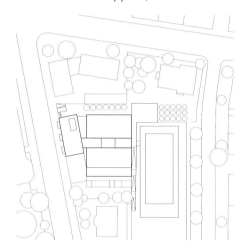

The Herz-Jesu church hall, built in 1970, is close, both spatially and in its design, to the new Herz-Jesu church (see DETAIL 2/2001) and the old rectory, which dates back to the Wilhelminian period. The church hall was renovated because it no longer fulfilled today's requirements. The aims were to correct the defects in the building substance and fire protection, and the functional weakness of the communal areas. On the one hand, the spirit of the 70s architecture was to be retained, but on the other, the renovation work visible on the interior and exterior should be identifiable as belonging to the late 90s. The lowering of the open atrium to below ground level improved the lighting and natural ventilation of the surrounding rooms. The surfaces of the facade are all rendered in the same pigmented mineral rendering, emphasising the plastic form of the individual building cubes. After cleaning the concrete base, polystyrene rigid foam sheets were fixed to it and fitted with reinforcement and mesh. A silicate plaster was applied to this construction using a scraped finish.

◱ DETAIL 10/2002

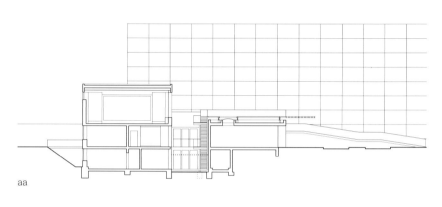

aa

Section · Floor plan
Scale 1:500

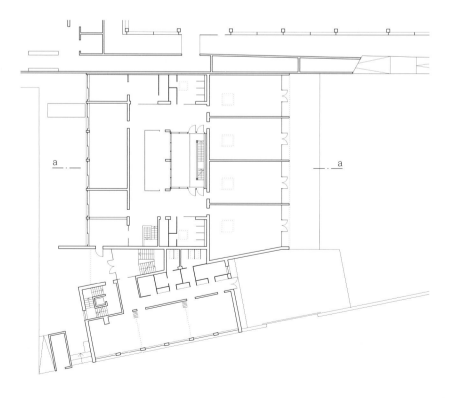

a

a

Vertical cross-section
Scale 1:20

1 ⌑ 30/6 mm steel sheet
2 ⌑ 30/10 mm steel sheet
3 Sunscreen, aluminium Z section
4 LJ 200 steel section
5 50 mm gravel
   plastic sealing sheet
   max. 180 mm rigid foam sheeting
   glass mat bituminous sealing layer
   perforated glass-fibre mat
   bitumen primer
6 HEA 200 steel section, primary beam
7 External thermal insulation composite system:
   8 mm pigmented silicate rendering with
   scraped finish 1.5 mm grain size with
   60 mm reinforcing mesh thermal insulation
   polystyrene
   120 mm parapet reinforced concrete
8 Corner protection rail

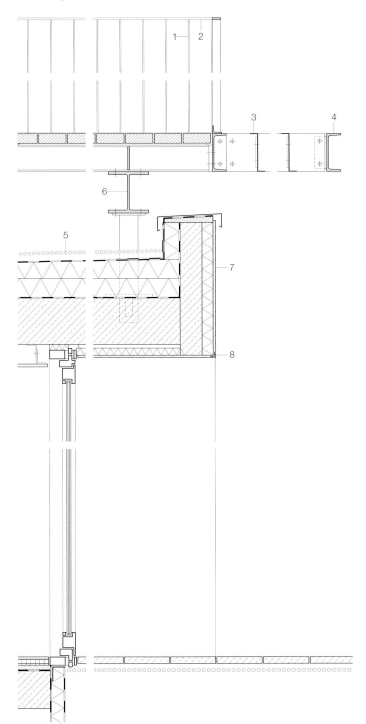

All Standards and Guidelines referred to this book are German or European Standards.

DIN EN 998-1, with its new classification of plastering and rendering mortars, has been the valid standard since September 2003. In parallel, the codes of practice in DIN 18 550 are still valid in Germany.

Classification for hardened mortar properties (Table 1, DIN EN 998-1)

Properties	Categories	Values
Compressive strength at 28 days	CS I CS II CS III CS IV	0.4–5.0 N/mm^2 1.5–5.0 N/mm^2 3.5–7.5 N/mm^2 $\geq$ 6 N/mm^2
Capillary water absorption[1]	W 0 W 1 W 2	Not specified, c $\leq$ 0.40 kg/m^{2}min^{0,5} c $\leq$ 0.20 kg/m^{2}min^{0,5}
Thermal conductivity	T 1 T 2	$\leq$ 0.1 W/mK $\leq$ 0.2 W/mK

[1] The previous standard unit of measurement kg/m^{2}h$^{0.5}$ has been changed to kg/m^{2}min$^{0.5}$.

Selected important parameters for comparison

Requirements for hardened mortars (Table 2, DIN EN 998-1)

No.	Test parameters	Method of testing	General purpose rendering/ plastering mortar GP	Lightweight rendering/ plastering mortar LW	Coloured rendering mortar CR	One coat rendering mortar for external use OC	Renovation mortar R	Thermal insulating mortar T
L2	Compressive strength (categories)	EN 1015-11[a]	CS I to CS IV	CS I to CS III	CS I to CS IV	CS I to CS IV	CS II	CS I to CS II
L5	Capillary water absorption (categories) (for mortars intended to be used in external elements)	EN 1015-18	W 0 to W 2	W 0 to W 2	W 0 to W 2	W 1 to W 2	$\geq$ 0.3 kg/m^2 after 24 h	W 1
L6	Water penetration after capillary water absorption test (in mm)	EN 1015-18	–	–	–	–	$\leq$ 5 mm	–
L8	Water vapour permeability coefficient (μ) (for mortars intended to be used in external elements)	EN 1015-19[a, b]	$\leq$ declared value	$\leq$ declared value	$\leq$ declared value	$\leq$ declared value	$\leq$ 15	$\leq$ 15

[a] For determination of storage conditions, the air lime content shall be calculated as Ca(OH)$_2$

[b] Test method EN 1015-19 determines water vapour permeance Λ (in kg/m^{2}sPa) whereas the value specified in this standard is the water vapour permeability coefficient μ.

The calculation of μ from Λ is given by the following formula:
$$\mu = \frac{1{,}94 \cdot 10^{-10}}{\Lambda}$$

$1{,}94 \cdot 10^{-10}$ corresponding to equivalent water vapour permeability factor in air at a temperature of 20 °C and atmospheric air pressure of 101 325 Pa.

Appendix
Mortar Mixing Ratios

According to DIN EN 998-1 it is no longer possible to lay down standard mixing ratios for mortar for all countries in Europe, due to the different regional building traditions and differences in the raw materials. The definition of mixing ratios (recipes) and fields of use shall therefore be based on the existing regional practices and experience. The German standard DIN 18 550 remains valid in this respect.

Mixing ratios by volume (Table 3, DIN 18 550 T 2)

Line	Mortar Group	Mortar Type	Mason's lime DIN 1061 Part 1						Building plasters with no additions added by the manufacturer			
			non-hydraulic lime hydrated hydraulic lime lime putty	hydraulic lime	hydraulic lime	eminently hydraulic lime	plaster, rendering + masonry binders DIN 4211	cement DIN 1164 part 1	anhydrous gypsum DIN 1168	plaster of Paris part 1	anhydrite binders DIN 4208	sand[1]
1	PI a	non-hydraulic lime mortar	1.0[2]									3.5–4.5
2				1.0[2]								3.0–4.0
3	PI b	hydraulic lime mortar	1.0									3.5–4.5
4				1.0								3.0–4.0
5	PI c	mortar with hydraulic lime				1.0						3
6	PII a	a mortar with eminently hydraulic lime or mortar with plaster, rendering and masonry binders				1.0 or	1.0					3.0–4.0
7	PII b	lime-cement mortar	1.5 or	2.0				1.0				9.0–11.0
8	PIII a	a cement mortar with hydraulic lime addition	≤ 0.5					2.0				6.0–8.0
9	PIII b	cement mortar						1.0				3.0–4.0
10	PIV a	a gypsum mortar							1.0[3]	1.0[3]		–
11	PIV b	sand gypsum mortar								1.0[3] or	1.0[3]	1.0–3.0
12	PIV c	gypsum-lime mortar	1.0 or	1.0					0.5–1.0 or	1.0–2.0		3.0–4.0
13	PIV d	lime-gypsum mortar	1.0 or	1.0					0.1–0.2 or	0.2–0.5		3.0–4.0
14	PV a	anhydrite mortar								1.0	≤ 2.5	
15	PV b	anhydrite lime mortar	1.0 or	1.5							3.0	12

[1] The values in this table are only valid for mineral aggregates with a dense structure.
[2] A limited addition of cement is allowed.
[3] White lime may be added in small amounts to improve the pliability. Retarders may be added to regulate the stiffening time.

The tables in DIN 18 550 are expected to be valid until 2005.
The nomenclature used is currently being changed in line with DIN EN 998-1.

External rendering systems (Table 3, DIN 18 550 T 1)

Line	Requirements and/or Used as	mortar group and/or type of coating material for base coat	finish coat[1]	admixture[2]
1		–	P I	
2		P I	P I	
3		–	P II	
4	no particular	P II	P I	
5	requirements	P II	P II	
6		P II	P Org. 1	
7		–	P Org. 1[3]	
8		–	P III	
9		P I	P I	required
10		–	P I c	required
11		–	P II	
12		P II	P I	
13	water-resistant	P II	P II	
14		P II	P Org 1	
15		–	P Org 1[3]	
16		–	P III[3]	
17		P I c	P I	required
18		P II	P I	required
19		–	P I c[4]	required[2]
20		–	P II[4]	
21	water-repellant[5]	P II	P II	required
22		P II	P Org 1	
23		–	P Org 1[3]	
24		–	P III[3]	
25		–	P II	
26		P II	P II	
27	increased strength	P II	P Org. 1	
28		–	P Org. 1[3]	
29		–	P III	
30	cellar wall exterior rendering	–	P III	
31		–	P III	
32	exterior plinth rendering	P III	P III	
33		P III	P Org 1	
34		–	P Org 1[3]	

[1] Finish coats of plaster/rendering can be textured or untextured (e.g. surfaces to be coated).

[2] Proof of suitability required (see DIN 18 550 part 2, issued January 1985, section 3.4)

[3] Only for concrete with a closed structure as a rendering base.

[4] Only permissible on plaster/rendering system with proof of suitability.

[5] Rubbed finish coats can require special measures.

Recommended grain sizes (Table 1, DIN 18 550 T 2)

Line	Use	Mortar for	grain size group or aggregate product size acc. to DIN 4226 part 1 in mm
1	exterior	machine-applied	0/4[1], (0/8)[1]
2	rendering	base coat	0/2, 0/4
3		finish coat	depending on technique
4	interior	machine-applied	0/4[1]
5	plasterwork	base coat	0/2, 0/4
6		finish coat	0/1, 0/2[2]

[1] The volume of coarse grains should be as large as possible.

[2] In decorative plasters/rendering, the coarse grain should be selected according to the plastering technique used.

Appendix
Interior plasterwork and mason's lime

Interior plaster systems (Table 3, DIN 18 550 T 1)

Line	Requirements and/or Used as	mortar group and/or type of coating material for base coat	finish coat[1]
1		–	P I a, b
2	only low loads	P I a, b	P I a, b
3		P II	P I a, b, P IV d
4		P IV	P I a, b, P IV d
5		–	P I c
6		P I c	P I c
7		–	P II
8		P II	P I c, P II, P IV a, b, c, P V, P Org. 1, P Org. 2
9		–	P III
10	usual loading[3]	P III	P I c, P II, P III, P Org. 1, P Org. 2
11		–	P IV a, b, c,
12		P IV a, b, c	P IV a, b, c, P Org. 1, P Org. 2
13		–	P V
14		P V[4]	P V, P Org 1, P Org. 2
15		–	P Org. 1, P Org. 2[4]
16		–	P I
17		P I	P I
18		–	P II
19	wet rooms[5]	P II	P I, P II, P Org. 1
20		–	P III
21		P III	P II, P III, P Org. 1
22		–	P Org. 1[4]

[1] If several mortar groups are named, only one may be used as a finish coat.

[2] Finish coats of plaster/rendering can be textured or untextured (e.g. surfaces to be coated).

[3] Including uses at low loads.

[4] Only for concrete with a closed structure as a rendering base.

[5] This does not include domestic kitchens and bathrooms (see section 4.2.3.3).

Building limes according to DIN 1060, now DIN EN 459-1

Name	Material basis	Commercial forms	Processing
air lime in the form of white lime	limestone, $CaCO_3$ calcined to quicklime, $CaO \approx 800\ °C$ $CaCO_3 \rightarrow CaO + CO_2$	quicklime in the form of lump lump white lime, ground to pulverised lime hydraulic white lime white lime putty	– dry slake to hydraulic white lime powder or wet slake to white lime putty – process without slaking
air lime in the form of carbide limes	product of the production of ethylene, C_2H_2, from calcium carbonate CaC_2. $CaC_2 + 2H_2O \rightarrow C_2H_2 + Ca(OH)_2$	hydraulic carbide lime carbide lime putty	– process without slaking
air lime in the form of dolomitic lime	dolomitic stone, $CaCO_3 \cdot MgCO_3$ calcined	pulverised dolomitic lime pulverised hydraulic dolomitic lime	– hydration – process without slaking
hydrated hydraulic lime	Marly limestone, calcined, min. 10 % hydraulic components	Hydraulic finish lime Hydraulic lime	– hydration – process without slaking
hydraulic lime	Marly limestone, calcined, min. 15 % hydraulic components	hydraulic lime, powdered	– process without slaking
eminently hydraulic lime	Marly limestone, calcined with addition of hydraulic materials, non-hydraulic or hydrated hydraulic lime, as necessary with the addition of hydraulic materials	eminently hydraulic lime, powdered	– process without slaking

Plaster and rendering admixtures (AM), (Table 12 from „Putze in Bausanierung und Denkmalpflege" by Tanja Dettmeing)

Influenced properties	Purpose	Mode of action	Historical admixture	Synthetic admixture	Effect of overdosing
Porosity	• improve the workability • reduce the settled apparent density • increase the frost resistance • increase the vapour permeability • deposition of salts	changes the surface tension of the mixing water, causing formation of small, stable pores	blood	tensides	• increase the stickiness • poor workability
Water retaining potential	• prevent firing-on by early release of water to the background • improve the workability characteristics	physical binding of mixing water in admixture capable of swelling	wood fibres	cellulose	• increase the stickiness • poor workability • disturbance of the setting time and hardening
Strength	• prevent slipping from rendering base	physical binding of mixing water in admixture capable of swelling	betonite, starch	starch ether	• increase the stickiness • poor workability
Elasticity	• prevent crack formation	composite, formation of a "reinforcing skeleton"	animal hairs, straw, wood fibres	glass fibres, polymer fibres, cellulose fibres	• poor workability
Bond strength	• improve bonding with the background	adhesion	curd cheese, casein, blood	polymer dispersion	• increase the stickiness • poor workability
Water-repelling capability	• reduce the capillary absorption	increase the surface tension in the capillaries and therefore reduce the capillary apsorbtion	animal and vegetable fibres, oils, soaps	stearates, oleates, palmitates, silicone resins	• reduce the final strength
Setting time (retardation)	• increase the setting time and the pot life	slow down the binder reaction	gypsum, sugar, wine, lime water, borax, okra roots	fruit acids, phosphates, silicone fluorides, sucroses, lignosulphonates, hydrogen carboxylic acids	• accelerate the setting time • blooming • signs of expansion
Setting time (acceleration)	• shorten the setting time	accelerate the binder reaction and solidification	gypsum	chloride, aluminate, hydrogen-carbonate	• final strength too low • blooming • signs of expansion
Colour	• adjust the colour	distribution of the pigment in the binder matrix	charcoal, minerals, brick meal, stone meal	anorganic/ mineral and organic pigments	• bleeding • mottling

*Rainfall map to determine
the average annual rainfall.*

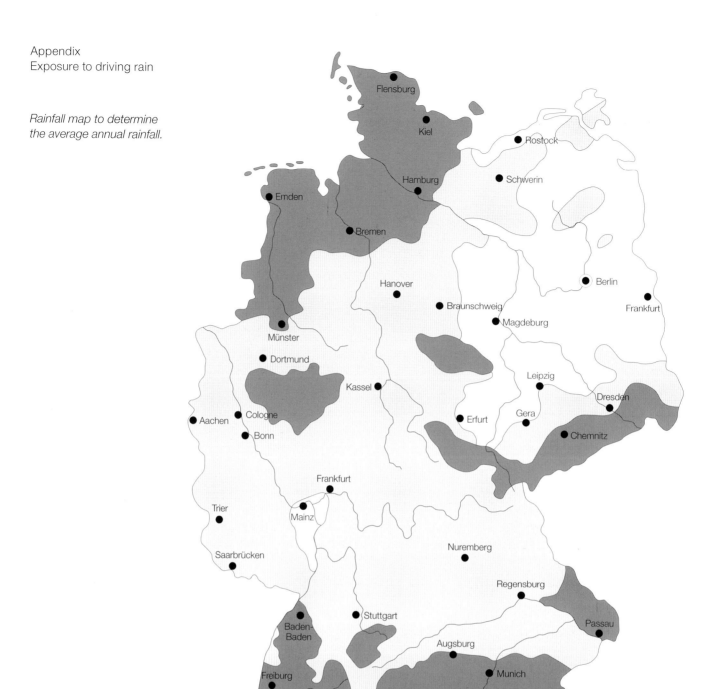

Annual rainfall:

☐ less than 600 mm

☐ between 66 and 800 mm

■ more than 800 mm
In the (windy) coastal areas of northern Germany:
more than 700 mm

The exposure of buildings or parts of buildings to driving rain
(exposure groups I, II or III according to the Frauenhofer Institute for Building Physics in Holzkirchen, Germany).

Exposure group I,   low exposure to driving rain:
areas with an annual rainfall of less than 600 mm, sites particularly well protected from the wind in areas with a higher annual rainfall.

Exposure group II,   medium exposure to driving rain:
areas with an annual rainfall between 600 and 800 mm and sites protected from the wind in areas with a higher annual rainfall: high-rise buildings and buildings on exposed sites in areas which would normally be assigned to the low exposure group according to the regional rain and wind patterns.

Exposure group III   high exposure to driving rain:
areas with an annual rainfall of over 800 mm and windy areas with a lower annual rainfall (e.g. coastal regions, upland and mountainous regions, alpine foothills). High-rise buildings and buildings on exposed sites in areas which would normally be assigned to the medium exposure group according to the regional rain and wind patterns

Suitability of the coating material on different plasters (Table 3, information sheet for painters)

No.	Coating materials	Mortar group acc. to DIN 18 550					
		P I a/b non-hydraulic lime hydrated hydraulic lime	P I c hydrated lime mortar	P II a/b lime cement	P III cement cement lime	P IV b gypsum — only on exterior surfaces protected from damp	P IV d lime-gypsum mortar — only on exterior surfaces protected from damp
1.	silicate paints	+	+	+	+	−	−
2.	emulsion type silicate paints	+	+	+	+	+	+
3.	silicone resin emulsion paints	+	+	+	+	+	+
4.	lime cement textured coatings	−	+	+	+	−	−
5.	silicate silicone resin emulsion textured coatings	+	+	+	+	+	+
6.	synthetic resin plaster acc. to DIN 18 558	−	−	+	+	+	−
7.	emulsion paints, weatherproof	−	−/+	+	+	+	−
8.	emulsion varnishes	−	−	+	+	+	−
9.	polymerizate resin paints	−	−	+	+	+	−
10.	calcimine (pit lime)	+	+	+	+	+	+

+ suitable
− unsuitable

Remarks: Textured coatings are coatings with a plaster-like appearance made from silicates, silicone resin emulsions or synthetic-resin modified lime cement, acc. to DIN 18558.

                         Plaster or rendering which contains lime or cement reacts in an alkaline manner in contact with moisture. Sustained neutralisation is not possible. The chosen coating materials must therefore be alkali-resistant.

Appendix
Testing and preparation of the background

Testing and treatment of the rendering base for coatings on exterior rendering (Table 2, Information sheet 9, Guidelines for painters)

Testing for	Test method	Detection	Technical notes and measures to be taken
Moisture	Visual inspection and scratch test	Damp spots, discoloured edges show	Treat the cause, allow to dry
Surface strength	Scratch test with a strong, angular object	The surface is damage if gentle pressure is used	Remove loose or friable parts manually or by machine. Soft layers are not a stable base for coatings
	Rub with hand	Little rubbing-off	If the surface of the plaster does not rub off easily, treat with plaster-hardening primer
		Heavy, deep rubbing-off	Not suitable for coating, renew the plaster
	Scratch test after wetting until the surface is saturated	The wetting softens the surface	Renew unstable plaster
Sintered layers	Scratch or grind the surface, carry out a wetting test with water	When dry, surface sheen, low absorbency. After wetting, darkening of the scratch or grinding marks	Remove manually or by machine and fluate where appropriate
Absorbency	Wetting test with water	Water does not penetrate the surface or water is only absorbed slowly and the surface becomes darker. Water forms beads.	Find cause and treat as necessary
		If the surface is highly absorbent the water is absorbed and the surface turns dark quickly	Strongly absorbent surfaces or surfaces which have a patchy pattern of different absorbencies should be treated with an equalisation primer.
Blooming	Visual inspection	Mostly white salts or calcium carbonate blooming	Remove source of moisture then allow to dry and remove the dry salts (brush off)
Moss, algae, mould	Visual inspection	Green or dark-coloured growth	Treat mechanically or chemically or remove using a high-pressure hot water jet. Follow up by treating
Cracks	Visual inspection	Crack appearance	Depending on the type and size of crack take suitable renovation measures
Dirt	Visual inspection		Remove
Rust spots	Visual inspection	Rust-discolouration of individual spots	Find cause and treat as necessary
Sites in need of repair	Visual inspection	Differences in texture	Equalise the textured finish. Fluate as necessary for subsequent coatings
Damaged areas	Visual inspection and tapping with hammer	Non-bonded plaster sounds hollow	Repair damaged areas

All paints and varnishes can be compared and classified by their building physical properties according to the draft standard EN 1062-1.

Example of the designation for a gloss coating with a dry film thickness of 50 μm to 100 μm, fine grain, water vapour transmission rate > 15 g/(m²d), liquid water permeability > 0.1 kg/(m²h^{0,5}) to 0.5 kg/(m²h^{0,5}) and no requirements for crack-bridging and carbon dioxide permeability.

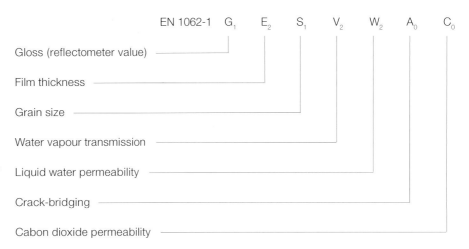

Gloss (reflectometer value)

Film thickness

Grain size

Water vapour transmission

Liquid water permeability

Crack-bridging

Cabon dioxide permeability

Classes for water vapour transmission rate (V) (Table 4, EN 1062-1)

Class		Requirements g/(m²d)	m^a
V_0			No requirement
V_1	high	> 150	< 0.14
V_2	medium	≤ 150 > 15	≥ 0.14 < 1.4
V_3	low	≤ 15	≥ 1.4

This property is used to assess the influence of the coating system on the humidity behaviour of the substrate.

[a] Values for diffusion-equivalent air thickness (s_d) in accordance with EN ISO 7783-2

Classes for liquid water permeability (w) (Table 5, EN 1062-1)

Class		Requirements kg/(m²h^{0,5})
w_0		No requirement
w_1	high	> 0.5
w_2	medium	≤ 0.5 > 0.1
w_3	low	≤ 0.1

This property is used to asses the influence of the coating system on water penetration.

Classes for carbon dioxide permeability (C) (Table 7, EN 1062-1)

Klasse	Requirements g/(m²d)	m^a
C_0	No requirements	No requirements
C_1	< 5	> 50

[a] values for diffusion equivalent air thickness (s_d) in accordance with EN 1062-6

Dark-coloured coatings can lead to a higher surface temperature (up to around 80 °C) on the exterior of windows or exterior doors. The warming of the surface can lead to increased discharge of resin in resinous softwoods. For this reason, the use of dark coatings on resinous softwoods on the exterior is not recommended. An increase in surface temperature leads to a significant drying-out of the coated wood and therefore to increased cracking. To prevent this, woods less susceptible to cracking should be used.

The given surface temperatures are measured values. Since the warming of the surface depends on various factors and is dependent on the time of day, the season and the geographic location, the values cannot be viewed as absolute, but should be considered as relative values.

The classification of the colours as either light, medium or dark includes some overlapping.

The surface temperatures of exterior rendering also increase if the rendering is dark coloured and can lead to the same physical effects. The temperatures are somewhat lower, compared to wood, such that black rendering has a surface temperature of up to 64 °C. To prevent cracks, reinforcing mesh must be used.

Surface temperatures for covering coatings
Table 2.6.1., Information Sheet 18, Technical Guidelines for Painters

RAL hue no.	hue	Surface temperature (°C)	Shade
9001	White	40–50	light shade
1004	Golden yellow		
1015	Light ivory		
2002	Vermilion	50–65	medium shade
3000	Flame red		
3003	Ruby red	65–80	dark shade
5007	Brilliant blue		
5010	Gentian blue		
6001	Reseda green		
7001	Silver grey		
7011	Iron grey		
7031	Blue grey		
8003	Clay brown		
9005	Jet black		

Surface temperatures for scumble coatings,
Table 2.6.2., Information sheet 18, Technical Guidelines for Painters

Scumbles	Surface temperature (°C)	Shade
"Natural" Light brown "Oak"	50–60	light shade
Medium red Medium brown "Teak"	60–70	medium shade
"Nut" Dark brown Anthracite	70–80	dark shade

Atmospheric corrosivity – categories and examples of typical environments (Table 1, DIN EN ISO 12944-2)

Corrosivity category	Thickness loss* after first year of exposure [µm]		Examples of typical environments		Film thickness Coating
	Low-carbon steel	Zinc	Exterior	Interior	
C 1 insignificant	≤ 1.3	≤ 0.1	–	insulated buildings ≤ 60 % rel. humidity	
C 2 low	> 1.3–25	> 0.1–0.7	Atmospheres with low levels of pollution, dry climate, e. g. rural areas	uninsulated buildings where condensation may occur, e. g. depots, sports halls	160 µm
C 3 medium	> 25–50	> 0.7–2.1	Urban and industrial atmospheres, moderate SO_2 pollution or coastal areas with low salinity	Rooms with high relative humidity and some air pollution, e. g. breweries, laundries, dairies	160–200 µm
C 4 high	> 50–80	> 2.1–4.2	Industrial areas and coastal areas with moderate salinity	Swimming pools, chemical plants, coastal ship and boatyards	200–320 µm
C 5 very high I (I = industry)	> 80–200	> 4.2–8.4	Industrial areas with high relative humidity and aggressive atmosphere	Buildings or areas with almost permanent condensation and with high levels of pollution	240–320 µm
C 5 very high M (M = marine)	> 80–200	> 4.2–8.4	Coastal and offshore areas with high, almost permanent condensation	Buildings or areas with high salinity and high levels of pollution	280–320 µm

* also given as mass loss [g/m²]
  100 µ equal 0.1 mm

Corrosion protection of steel structures under atmospheric conditions using protective paint systems, based on DIN EN ISO 12944-5. Preparation of the surface: Sa 2 1/2 (DIN EN ISO 12944-4) and roughness R_{y5} 40 to < 80 µm (DIN EN ISO 8503-1)

Syst.-No.	Primer	Film thickness [µm]	Intermediate and/or top coat	Film thickness [µm]	Number of coats	Top coats	Film thickness [µm]	Number of coats	Film thickness [µm] (System)
1	AK zinc phosphate	100			1–2	AK	60	1	160
2	EP zinc dust	60	AY-Hydro	100	2–3				160
3	EP zinc phosphate	160			1–2				160
4	AK zinc phosphate	100			1–2	AK	100	1–2	200
5	AY-Hydro-zinc phosphate	120			1–2	AK, AY, PVC	80	1–2	200
6	EP zinc dust	60	EP, PUR	100	2–3				160
7	EP zinc phosphate	80	EP, PUR	120	2–3				200
8	EP zinc dust	60	AY-Hydro	80	2	AY, PVC	60	1	200
9	EP zinc dust	80	EP, PUR	100	2–3	PUR	60	1	240
10	EP zinc dust	80	AY-Hydro	100	2–3	AY, PVC	60	1	240
11	EP zinc phosphate	160	EP, PUR	120	2–4				280
12	EP zinc dust	80	EP, PUR	160	2–3	PUR	80	1–2	320
13	EP zinc phosphate	80	EP, PUR	160	2–3	PUR	80	1–2	320

The rightmost section of the table lists Corrosivity category columns (C2, C3, C4, C5-I, C5-M), each subdivided into short / medium / long, with shaded cells indicating applicability.

- Top and intermediate coats with or without micaceous iron pigments
- In interior spaces, EP top coats can be used in place of PUR top coats
- For EP, also EP combinations, if these are proven to be equivalent
- In place of EP zinc dust, 1 K PUR zinc dust and 1 K/2 ESI zinc dust (relative humidity during working and hardening 50 %)
  However, only ESI zinc dust if no second coating is intended in the workshop or if a system with a higher temperature resistance (up to 400 °C) is required

Plaster/Rendering

DIN EN 413-1 (in preparation) issue: 2004-05
Masonry cement – Part 1: Composition,
specifications and conformity criteria;
German edition EN 413-1 2004

DIN EN 459-1 issue: 2002-02
Building lime – Part 1: Definitions, specifications and conformity criteria;
German edition EN 459-1: 2001

DIN EN 459-2 issue: 2002-02
Building lime – Part 2: Test methods;
German edition EN 459-2: 2001

DIN EN 459-3 issue: 2002-02
Building lime – Part 3: Conformity evaluation

DIN EN 998-1 issue: 2003-09
Specification of mortar for masonry –
Part 1: Rendering and plastering mortar

DIN EN 998-2 issue: 2003-09
Specification of mortar for masonry –
Part 2: Masonry mortar

DIN 4121 issue: 1978-07
Suspended wire-plaster ceilings; plaster
ceilings with metal lathing, Rabitz ceilings,
specifications for construction

DIN 4208 issue: 1997-04 Anhydrite binder

DIN 1164 issue: 2000-11
Cement with special properties – composition,
specifications, proof of conformity

DIN 1168-1 issue: 1986-01
Building plasters; Nomenclature, types and
uses; delivery and labelling

DIN 1168-2 issue: 1975-07 Building plasters;
Specifications, test methods, monitoring

DIN 1169 Loam mortar for masonry, plastering
and rendering

DIN EN 13279-1 (draft), issue: 1998-07
Gypsum and gypsum based building plaster –
Part 1: Definitions and requirements

DIN EN 13279-2 (draft) issue:
1998-07 Gypsum and gypsum based building
plaster – Part 2: Test methods

DIN EN 13658-1 (draft),
issue: 1999-10
Metal laths and beading –
Definitions, requirements and test methods.
– Part 1: Internal plastering

DIN EN 13658-2 (draft),
issue: 1999-11
Metal laths and beading –
Definitions, requirements and test methods.
– Part 2: External rendering

DIN EN 13914-1 (draft),
issue: 2000-12 The design, preparation and
application of external rendering and internal
plastering – Part 1: External rendering

DIN EN 13914-2 (draft),
issue: 2002-07
The design, preparation and application of
external rendering and internal plastering –
Part 2: Internal plastering

DIN 18180 issue: 1989-09 Plasterboard;
Types, specifications, test methods

DIN 18350 issue: 2002-12
German Construction Contract Procedures
(VOB) – Part C: General technical terms of
contract for constrution works (ATV);
rendering, plastering and stucco

DIN 18 550-1 issue: 1985-01 Plaster and
rendering; Nomenclature and requirements.
This standard is to be superseded by
DIN EN 13914-1

DIN 18 550-2 issue: 1985-01 Plaster and
rendering; Plaster and rendering made from
mortars with mineral binders; application.

DIN 18 550-3 issue: 1991-03 Plaster and
rendering; Thermally insulating plaster systems
using mortar with mineral binders and expanded polystyrene (EPS) as an aggregate.

DIN 18 550-4 issue: 1993-08 Plaster and
rendering; lightweight plaster; application.

DIN 18 555 Testing of mortars with mineral
binders

DIN 18 556 issue: 1985-01 Testing of
coating materials for synthetic resin plasters
and of synthetic resin plasters

DIN 18557 Factory-made mortar; Manufacture,
monitoring and delivery

DIN 18 558 issue: 1985-01 Synthetic resin
plasters; definitions, specifications, applications

DIN 18559 issue: 1988-2 External thermal
insulation composite systems

Draft WTA (International Association for Science
and Technology of Building Maintenance and
Monuments Preservation) information sheet
"Lime plaster for the preservation of monuments"

WTA information sheet 8-6-99/D "Restoration of
timbered buildings according to the WTA, coatings on timber-frame walls – nogging/plasters"

WTA information sheet 2-2-91/D "Renovation
plaster systems"

WTA information sheet 2-2-99/D "Supplement to
WTA information sheet 2-2-91/D"

WTA information sheet 2-4-94/D "Evaluation
and restoration of cracked rendering on
facades"

Paints

DIN EN 971-1 + supplement 1 issue: 1996-09
Paints and varnishes, terms and definitions for
coating materials – Part 1: General terms

DIN EN 927-1 (5 Parts) issue: 1996-10 Paints
and varnishes – coating materials and coating
systems for exterior woodwork
– Part 1: Classification and selection

DIN EN 1062-1 (draft) issue: 2002-10
Coating materials – coating materials and
coating systems for exterior mineral substrates
and concrete – Part 1: Classification

DIN EN 1062-3 issue: 1999-02 Paints and
varnishes – coating materials and coating
systems for exterior mineral substrates
and concrete – Part 3: Determination and
classification of liquid-water transmission rate
(permeability)

DIN EN 1062-6 issue: 2002-10 Coating materials
– coating materials and coating systems for
exterior mineral substrates and concrete –
Part 6: Determination of carbon dioxide
permeability

DIN EN 1062-7 (draft) issue: 2002-10
Coating materials – coating materials and
coating systems for exterior mineral substrates
and concrete – Part 7: Determination of
crack-bridging properties

DIN EN 1062-11 issue: 2002-10 Coating materials
– coating materials and coating systems for
exterior mineral substrates and concrete –
Part 11: Methods of conditioning before testing

DIN EN ISO 4618-2 issue: 1999-07 Paints and
varnishes – terms and definitions for coating
materials – Part 2: Special terms relating to
paint characteristics and properties

DIN EN ISO 4618-3 issue: 1999-07 Paints and
varnishes, terms and definitions for coating
materials – Part 3: Surface preparation and
methods of application

DIN 6164 (3 parts + supplement): DIN colour
cards

DIN EN ISO 7783-1 issue: 1999-06
Coating materials – determination of water
vapour transmission rate – Part 1 dish method
for free films

DIN EN ISO 7783-2 issue: 1999-04
Paints and varnishes – coating materials and
coating systems for exterior mineral substrates
and concrete – Part 2: Determination and classification of water-vapour transmission rate
(permeability) (ISO 7783-2: 1999)

DIN EN ISO 12944-5 issue:1998-07
Paints and varnishes. Corrosion protection of
steel structures using protective paint systems.
Part 5: Protective paint systems

DIN 18363 issue: 2002-12 German Construction
Contract Procedures (VOB) – Part C: General
technical terms of contract for construction
work (ATV); painting and varnishing work

DIN 18364 issue: 2000-12 German Construction
Contract Procedures (VOB) – Part C: General
technical terms of contract for construction
work (ATV); corrosion protection of steel and
aluminium structures

DIN 53220 issue: 1978-04 Paints and similar
coating materials; used to coat a surface;
definitions and influencing factors

DIN 53778-3 issue: 1983-08 Polymer dispersion
paints; Specification of the contrast ratio
and brightness of the paints

DIN 55943 issue: 2001-10
Colouring matters – Definitions

DIN 55944: issue: 2003-11 Colouring matters,
Classification according to coloristic and
chemical considerations

DIN 55945 issue: 1999-07 Paints and varnishes,
terms and definitions for coating materials and
coatings – terms and definitions additional to
DIN EN 971-1, DIN EN ISO 4618-2 and
DIN EN ISO 4618-3

DIN 55990 issue: 1979-12 Testing of paints and
similar coating materials

DIN EN 13300 issue: 2002-11 Coating materials
– coating materials which contain water and
coating systems for interior walls and ceilings
– classification

Plaster and rendering – Manufacturers/organisations

Manufacturers

alsecco Bauchemische Produkte
GmbH & Co KG
Kupferstraße 50
D-36208 Wildeck, Germany
Tel.: +49 (0) 36922 88-0
Fax: +49 (0) 36922 88-330
www.alsecco.de

BaumitBayosan GmbH & Co. KG
Reckenberg 12
D-87541 Bad Hindelang, Germany
Tel.: +49 (0) 8324 921-0
Fax: +49 (0) 8324 921-470
www.bayosan.de

cd-color GmbH & Co. KG
Wetterstraße 58
D-58313 Herdecke, Germany
Tel.: +49 (0) 2330 926-0
Fax: +49 (0) 2330 926-171
www.cd-color.de
www.doerken.de

Colfirmit Rajasil GmbH & Co. KG
Thölauer Straße 25
D-95603 Marktredwitz, Germany
Tel.: +49 (0) 9231 802-0
Fax: +49 (0) 9231 802-330
www.colfirmit.de

Daxorol Putz und Farben GmbH
Zum Tauberg 9
D-57334 Bad Laasphe-Feudingen,
Germany
Tel.: +49 (0) 2754 3748-0
Fax: +49 (0) 2754 3748-24
www.daxorol.com

Deitermann Chemiewerk
GmbH & Co. KG
Lohstraße 61
D-45711 Datteln, Germany
Tel.: +49 (0) 2363 399-0
Fax: +49 (0) 2363 399-354
www.deitermann.de

FEMA Farben + Putze GmbH
Junkerstraße 3
D-76257 Ettlingen, Germany
Tel.: +49 (0) 7243 371-0
Fax: +49 (0) 7243 371-128
www.fema.de

Hasit Trockenmörtel
GmbH & Co. KG
Landshuter Straße 30
D-85356 Freising, Germany
Tel.: +49 (0) 8161 602-0
Fax: +49 (0) 8161 602-486
www.hasit.de

HeidelbergCement AG
Product group plaster systems
Berliner Straße 6
D-69120 Heidelberg, Germany
Tel.: +49 (0) 6221 481-251
Fax: +49 (0) 6221 481-700
www.hzag.de

Henkel Bautechnik GmbH
Ceresit
Erkrather Straße 230
D-40233 Düsseldorf, Germany
Tel.: +49 (0) 211 7379-0
Fax: +49 (0) 211 7379-299
www.henkel-bautechnik.de

Knauf Gips KG
Am Bahnhof 7
D-97343 Iphofen, Germany
Tel.: +49 (0) 9323 31-0
Fax: +49 (0) 9323 31-277
www.knauf.de

Kühn Putzunternehmen GmbH
Morsestraße 12
D-48432 Rheine, Germany
Tel.: +49 (0) 5971 964001
Fax: +49 (0) 5971 964002
www.kuehn-putz.de

Lafarge Gips GmbH
Frankfurter Landstraße 2–4
D-61440 Oberursel, Germany
Tel.: +49 (0) 6171 61020
Fax: +49 (0) 6171 61392
www.lafargegips.de

Marmorit GmbH
Ellighofen 6
D-79283 Bollschweil, Germany
Tel.: +49 (0) 7633 810-0
Fax: +49 (0) 7633 810-113
www.marmorit.de

Maxit Deutschland GmbH
Kupfertorstraße 35
D-79206 Breisach, Germany
Tel.: +49 (0) 7668 711-0
Fax: +49 (0) 7668 711-117
www.maxit.de

MC Bauchemie
Müller GmbH & Co.
Am Kruppwald 6–8
D-46238 Bottrop, Germany
Tel.: +49 (0) 2041 101-0
Fax: +49 (0) 2041 64017
www.mc-bauchemie.de

PCI Augsburg GmbH (degussa)
Piccardstraße 11
D-86159 Augsburg, Germany
Tel.: +49 (0) 821 5901-0
Fax. +49 (0) 821 5901-372
www.pci-augsburg.de

P E L I - GmbH
Oeynhausener Straße 42
D-32584 Löhne, Germany
Tel.: +49 (0) 5732 4000
Fax: +49 (0) 5732 16971
www.peli-putz.de

Protektorwerk
Florenz Maisch GmbH & Co. KG
Viktoriastraße 58
D-76571 Gaggenau, Germany
Tel.: +49 (0) 7225 977-0
Fax: +49 (0) 7225 977-180
www.protektor.com

quick-mix Gruppe
GmbH & Co. KG
Mühleneschweg 6
D-49090 Osnabrück, Germany
Tel.: +49 (0) 541 60101
Fax: +49 (0) 541 6018 53
www.quick-mix.de

Remmers GmbH & Co.
Chemische Baustoffe
Bernhard-Remmers-Straße 13
D-49624 Löningen, Germany
Tel.: +49 (0) 5432 83-0
Fax: +49 (0) 5432 3985
www.remmers.de

Rigips GmbH
Schanzenstraße 84
D-40549 Düsseldorf, Germany
Tel.: +49 (0) 211 5503-0
Fax: +49 (0) 211 5503-208
www.rigips.de

Saint-Gobain Weber GmbH
Clevischer Ring 127
D-51063 Cologne, Germany
Tel.: +49 (0) 221 6689-0
Fax: +49 (0) 221 6689-214
www.weber-broutin.de

Sakret Trockenbaustoffe Europa
GmbH & Co. KG
Otto-von-Guericke-Ring 3
D-65205 Wiesbaden, Germany
Tel.: +49 (0) 6122 9138-0
Fax: +49 (0) 6122 9138-18
www.sakret.de

Schaefer Krusemark
GmbH & Co. KG
Louise-Seher-Straße 6
D-65582 Diez/Lahn, Germany
Tel.: +49 (0) 6432 503-0
Fax: +49 (0) 6432 503-119
www.schaefer-krusemark.de

Schomburg GmbH
Wiebuschstraße 2-8
D-32760 Detmold, Germany
Tel.: +49 (0) 5231 953-00
Fax: +49 (0) 5231 953-123
www.schomburg.de

Schwarzwälder Edelputzwerk GmbH
Industriestraße 10
D-77833 Ottersweier, Germany
Tel.: +49 (0) 7223 9836-0
Fax: +49 (0) 7223 9836-90
www.schwepa.com

Schwenk Putztechnik
GmbH & Co. KG
Hindenburgring 15
D-89077 Ulm, Germany
Tel.: 0731 9341-0
Fax: 0731 9341 388
www.schwenk.de

SOTANO Mörtel und Putze
GmbH + Co. KG
Mendener Straße 40
D-58675 Hemer
Tel.: +49 (0) 2372 927151
Fax: +49 (0) 2372 927159
www.sotano.de

Organisations

Bundesverband der
Gipsindustrie e.V.
D-64295 Darmstadt, Germany
Tel.: +49 (0) 6151 36682-0
Fax: +49 (0) 6151 36682-22
www.gips.de

Bundesverband der Deutschen
Kalkindustrie e.V.
Annastraße 67–71
D-50968 Cologne, Germany
Tel.: +49 (0) 221 934674-0
Fax: +49 (0) 221 934674-10
www.kalk.de

Bundesverband der Deutschen
Zementindustrie e.V.
Pferdmengesstraße 7
D-50968 Cologne, Germany
Tel.: +49 (0) 221 37656-0
Fax: +49 (0) 221 37656-86
www.bdzement.de

Dachverband Lehm e.V.
PO Box 1172
D-99409 Weimar, Germany
Tel.: +49 (0) 3643 778349
Fax: +49 (0) 3643 77 83 50
www.dachverband-lehm.de

Deutsche Bauchemie e.V.
Karlstraße 21
D-60329 Frankfurt a. Main, Germany
Tel.: +49 (0) 69 2556-1318
Fax: +49 (0) 69 251609
www.deutsche-bauchemie.de

Deutscher Stuckgewerbebund
im Zentralverband des Deutschen
Baugewerbes
Kronenstraße 55–58
D-10117 Berlin, Germany
Tel.: +49 (0) 30 20314-5 22
Fax: +49 (0) 30 20314-5 83
stuck@zdb.de

Fachgemeinschaft
Kunstharzputze e.V.
D-40237 Düsseldorf, Germany
Tel.: +49 (0) 211 6793173
Fax: +49 (0) 211 6793173
www.kunstharzputze.de

Fachverband Kies, Sand, Splitt,
Mörtel und Transportbeton
Prinzessinnenstraße 8
D-10969 Berlin, Germany
Tel.: +49 (0) 30 616957-30
Fax: +49 (0) 30 616957-40
fano-berlin@t-online.de

Fachverband Wärmedämm-
Verbundsysteme e.V.
Fremersbergstraße 33
D-76530 Baden-Baden, Germany
Tel.: +49 (0) 7221 300989-0
Fax: +49 (0) 7221 300989-9
www.fachverband-wdvs.de

Hauptverband Farbe, Gestaltung,
Bautenschutz
Hahnstraße 70
D-60528 Frankfurt a. Main, Germany
Tel.: +49 (0) 69 66575-300
Fax: +49 (0) 69 66575-350
www.farbe.de

Industrieverband WerkMörtel e.V.
Haus der Baustoffindustrie
Düsseldorfer Straße 50
D-47051 Duisburg, Germany
Tel.: +49 (0) 203 99239-0
Fax: +49 (0) 203 99239-90
www.iwm-info.de

NCS COLOUR CENTRE
Europäisches Color Centrum
Bayreuther Straße 8
D-10787 Berlin, Germany
Tel.: +49 (0) 30 210901-0
Fax: +49 (0) 30 21473671
www.ncscolour.de

Paint – Manufacturers

Akzo Nobel Deco GmbH
Werner-von-Siemens-Straße 11
D-31515 Wunstorf, Germany
Tel.: +49 (0) 5031 961-0
Fax: +49 (0) 5031 961-274
www.akzonobel.de

Alligator Farbwerke GmbH
Markstraße 203
D-32130 Enger, Germany
Tel.: +49 (0) 5224 930-0
Fax. +49 (0) 5224 7881
www.alligator.de

Alpina Farben
Vertriebs-GmbH & Co. KG
Roßdörfer Straße 50
Administration:
Dr. Robert Murjahn-Straße 13
D-64372 Ober-Ramstadt, Germany
Tel.: +49 (0) 6154 71-0
Fax: +49 (0) 6154 71-632
www.alpina-farben.de

AURO Pflanzenchemie AG
Alte Frankfurter Straße 211
D-38122 Braunschweig, Germany
Tel.: +49 (0) 531 28141-0
Fax: +49 (0) 531 28141-61
www.auro.de

BASF Coatings AG
Glasuritstraße 1
D-48165 Münster, Germany
Tel.: +49 (0) 2501 14-0
Fax: +49 (0) 2501 14-3373
www.basf-coatings.de

Beeck'sche Farbwerke Beeck
GmbH & Co. KG
Burgauerstraße 2
D-70597 Stuttgart, Germany
Tel.: +49 (0) 711 900-200
Fax: +49 (0) 711 900-2010
www.beeck.de

Biofa-Naturprodukte W. Hahn GmbH
Dobelstraße 22
D-73087 Boll, Germany
Tel.: +49 (0) 7164 9405-0
Fax: +49 (0) 7164 9405-96
www.biofa.de

Brillux GmbH & Co. KG
Weseler Straße 401
D-48163 Münster, Germany
Tel.: +49 (0) 251 7188-0
Fax: +49 (0) 251 7188-439
www.brillux.de

Caparol Farben Lacke
Bautenschutz GmbH
Roßdörfer Straße 50
Industriegebiet 1
D-64372 Ober-Ramstadt, Germany
Tel.: +49 (0) 6154 71-0
Fax: +49 (0) 6154 71-1391
www.caparol.de

Chemische Fabrik Harold Scholz
GmbH & Co. KG
Partensteiner Straße 105–107
D-97816 Lohr a. M., Germany
Tel.: +49 (0) 9352 8748-0
Fax: +49 (0) 9352 8748-22
www.harold-scholz.de

Dinova GmbH & Co. KG
Bachstraße 38
D-53639 Königswinter, Germany
Tel.: +49 (0) 2223 72-0
Fax: +49 (0) 2223 287-54
www.dinova.de

Dracholin GmbH
Paints • Coloured rendering
Composite insulation systems
Carl-Zeiss-Straße 19
D-72555 Metzingen, Germany
Tel.: +49 (0) 7123 9656-0
Fax: +49 (0) 7123 41652
www.dracholin.de

einzA Lackfabrik GmbH
Rotenhäuser Straße 10
D-21109 Hamburg, Germany
Tel.: +49 (0) 40 751007-0
Fax: +49 (0) 40 751007 67
www.einza.com

Europäisches Color Centrum GmbH
Bayreuther Straße 8
D-10787 Berlin, Germany
Tel.: +49 (0) 30 210901-25
Fax: +49 (0) 30 21473671
www.ncsclour.de

G. E. Habich's Söhne
Farbenfabriken
Burgstraße 3
D-34359 Reinhardshagen
Tel.: +49 (0) 5544 791-0
Fax: +49 (0) 5544 8238

Glasurit GmbH
Glasuritstraße 1
D-48165 Münster-Hiltrup, Germany
Tel.: +49 (0) 2501 14-0
Fax: +49 (0) 2501 14-3373
www.glasurit.de

griwecolor
Farben und Beschichtungen GmbH
Wieselbrunnen 2
D-78199 Bräunlingen-Döggingen,
Germany
Tel.: +49 (0) 7707 9904-0
Fax: +49 (0) 7707 9904-50
www.griwecolor.de

Herbol
Akzo Nobel Deco GmbH
– Business Area Professional –
Vitalisstraße 198–226
D-50827 Cologne, Germany
Tel.: +49 (0) 221 5881-0
Fax: +49 (0) 221 5881-335
www.herbol.de

imparat Farbwerk Iversen & Mähl
GmbH & Co. KG
Hauptwerk Glinde
Siemensstraße 8
D-21509 Glinde/Hamburg, Germany
Tel.: +49 (0) 40 727708-0
Fax: +49 (0) 40 727708-70
www.imparat.de

IRSA Lackfabrik
Irmgard Sallinger GmbH
An der Günz 15
D-86489 Deisenhausen, Germany
Tel.: +49 (0) 8282 8944-0
Fax: +49 (0) 8282 8944-44
www.irsa.de

Karl Klenk GmbH & Co.
Farben- und Lackfabrik
Weissacher Straße 66–68
D-71522 Backnang, Germany
Tel.: +49 (0) 7191 181-0
Fax: +49 (0) 7191 63608
www.bakolor.de

Keimfarben GmbH & Co. KG
Keimstraße 16
D-86420 Diedorf, Germany
Tel.: +49 (0) 821 4802-0
Fax: +49 (0) 821 4802-210
www.keimfarben.de

Kremer Pigmente
Farbmühle
Hauptstraße 41–47
D-88317 Aichstetten/Allgäu,
Germany
Tel.: +49 (0) 7565 1011
Fax: +49 (0) 7565 1606
www.kremer-pigmente.de

Livos Pflanzenchemie
GmbH & Co. KG
Auengrund 10
D-29568 Wieren, Germany
Tel.: +49 (0) 5825 88-0
Fax: +49 (0) 5825 8860
www.livos.de

Meffert AG Farbwerke ProfiTec
Sandweg 15
D-55543 Bad Kreuznach, Germany
Tel.: +49 (0) 671 870-0
Fax: +49 (0) 671 870-392
www.profitec.de

Muster-Schmidt KG
RAL-colour card sales
Schuhstraße
D-37154 Sudheim, Germany
Tel.: +49 (0) 5551 90842-0
Fax: +49 (0) 5551 90842-29
www.muster-schmidt.de

Paul Jaeger GmbH & Co. KG
Lackfabrik
Siemens Straße 6
D-71696 Möglingen, Germany
Tel.: +49 (0) 7141 2444-0
Fax: +49 (0) 7141 2444-44
www.jaegerlacke.de

Relius Coatings GmbH & Co. KG
Donnerschweer Straße 372
D-26123 Oldenburg, Germany
Tel.: +49 (0) 441 3402-0
Fax: +49 (0) 441 3402-358
www.relius.de

Rudolf Hensel GmbH
Lauenburger Landstraße 11
D-21039 Börnsen, Germany
Tel.: +49 (0) 40 721062-10
Fax: +49 (0) 40 721062-52
www.rudolf-hensel.de

Schulz GmbH
Farben- und Lackfabrik
An der Altnah
D-55450 Langenlonsheim, Germany
Tel.: +49 (0) 6704 9388-0
Fax: +49 (0) 6704 9388-50
www.schulz-farben.de

Seitz + Kerler GmbH & Co. KG
Friedenstraße 5–8
D-97816 Lohr a. M., Germany
Tel.: +49 (0) 9352 87870
Fax: +49 (0) 9352 8787-11
www.seilo.de

Sigma Coatings
Farben- und Lackwerke GmbH
Klüsenerstraße 54
D-44805 Bochum, Germany
Tel.: +49 (0) 234 869-0
Fax: +49 (0) 234 869-358
www.sigma-coatings.de

Silinwerk van Baerle & Co.
D-64579 Gernsheim, Germany
Tel.: +49 (0) 6258 940-0
Fax: +49 (0) 6258 2561
www.silin.com

Sto AG
Ehrenbachstraße 1
D-79780 Stühlingen, Germany
Tel.: +49 (0) 7744 57-1010
Fax: +49 (0) 7744 57-2010
www.sto.de

Uzin Utz AG
Dieselstraße 3
D-89079 Ulm, Germany
Po box 4080
D-89030 Ulm, Germany
Tel.: +49 (0) 731 4097-0
Fax: +49 (0) 731 4097-110
www.uzin-utz.com

Wacker-Chemie GmbH
Hanns-Seidel-Platz 4
D-81737 Munich, Germany
Tel.: +49 (0) 89 6279-01
Fax: +49 (0) 89 6279-1770
www.wacker.com

Wema Flüssigtapete
Jurastraße 8
D-96146 Altendorf/Seußling,
Germany
Tel.: +49 (0) 9545 7 06 41
Fax: +49 (0) 9545 53 21
www.wema-flüssigtapete.de

Wulff GmbH & Co. KG
Niederlassung Lingen
Schillerstraße 27
D-49811 Lingen, Germany
Tel.: +49 (0) 591 71003-0
Fax: +49 (0) 591 71003-60
www.wulff-gmbh.de

Subject Index

Bibliography:

Gips-Datenbuch
Bundesverband der Gipsindustrie e.V.
Darmstadt, 2003

Lehmbau Regeln
Dachverband Lehm e.V. (German Loam Association)
Verlag Vieweg, Weimar 1998

Putze für Bausanierung und Denkmalpflege
Tanja Dettmering, Helmut Kollmann
Verlag Bauwesen, Leipzig 2001

Malmaterial und seine Verwendung im Bilde
Max Doerner
Verlag Enke, Stuttgart 1994

Bautechnik, Fachkunde Bau
Europa Lehrmittel, Haan-Gruiten 1999

Der Baustoff Lehm – eine ökologische Alternative
Figgemeier, M.
WTA-Schriftenreihe XIR. 21,
Aedificatio-Verlag
Freiburg 2000

Technische Richtlinien
für Maler- und Lackiererarbeiten
Hauptverband Farbe
Frankfurt 2002

Praktische Bauphysik
Gottfried C. O. Lohmeyer
B.G. Teubner Verlag, Stuttgart 1995

Biologisch natürlich Bauen
Josef Kroiss, August Bammer
S. Hirzel Verlag, Stuttgart 2000

Außenputz
Helmut Künzel
Fraunhofer IRB Verlag, Stuttgart 2003

Mauerwerksatlas
Pfeifer, Ramcke, Achtziger, Zilch
Institut für internationale
Architektur-Dokumentation GmbH, Munich
Birkhäuser Verlag, Basel · Boston · Berlin 2001

Bautabellen für Ingenieure
Klaus-Jürgen Schneider
Werner-Verlag, Düsseldorf 1994

Handbuch Fassadendämmsysteme
Kai Schild, Michael Weyers
Fraunhofer IRB, Stuttgart 2003

Historische Beschichtungstechniken
Kurt Schönburg
Verlag Bauwesen, Leipzig 2002

Baustoffkenntnis, erweiterte Auflage
Wilhelm Stolz
Werner-Verlag, Düsseldorf 1995

Farben, Lacke, Beschichtungssysteme
Alban Wekenmann, DVA
Stuttgart-Munich 2002

Picture credits:

Rendering

Pages 31, 41 right:
Christine Köpke, Darmstadt, Germany

Page 34:
Batelle-Institut, Frankfurt/Main, Germany

Page 36 left, 42:
Bundesverband der Gipsindustrie e.V. (German Gypsum Industry Association), Darmstadt, Germany

Page 36 centre:
Maxit, Breisach, Germany
Page 36 right:
Heidelberger Zement, Heidelberg, Germany

Page 37 top figs. 1-6, 38 left, 44-45, 47-48, 49 left, 54 (70-80), 57 (1):
Weber-Broutin, Cologne, Germany

Page 37 bottom, 38 right, 52 (60-63), 55 bottom, 56 (1, 4), 57 (3-4) :
Joachim Raab, Frankfurt/Main, Germany

Page 38 centre, 39, 43, 49 right, 52 top left, 53 top left and centre, 54 (69):
Gerhard Neff, Darmstadt, Germany

Page 41 left, 55 top left:
J. + H. Klumpp, Stuttgart, Germany
Page 46 left:
Helmut Kollmann, Leipzig, Germany

Page 46 right:
Schomburg GmbH, Detmold, Germany

Page 50:
Schaefer-Krusemark GmbH & Co. KG, Diez/Lahn, Germany

Page 51:
Sto AG, Stühlingen, Germany

Page 52 bottom right, 53 bottom, 55 top centre and right, 56 (5):
Alexander Reichel, Kassel, Germany

Page 53 top right:
Keimfarben GmbH & Co.KG, Diedorf, Germany

Page 56 (2-3), 57 (2):
Irene Meissner, Munich, Germany

Paints

Page 61 left:
Freies Deutsches Hochstift,
Goethe-Museum, Frankfurt, Germany

Page 61 right, 65 left:
from: Margarete Bruns, Das Rätsel Farbe,
Philipp Reclam jun., Stuttgart 1997

Page 62 top left and right, 63 left and right, 78 left and centre:
Alexander Reichel, Kassel, Germany

Page 62 centre:
Gerhard Neff, Darmstadt, Germany

Page 63 centre, 66 right, 74 right:
Keimfarben GmbH & Co.KG, Diedorf, Germany

Page 64, 65 right, 66 left, 67-70, 73 top, 74 left, 75, 77:
Caparol Farben Lacke Bautenschutz GmbH,
D- Ober-Ramstadt, Germany

Page 71:
Hensel GmbH, Börnsen, Germany

Page 72, 73 left (430-32):
Sto AG, Stühlingen, Germany

Page 76:
Margherita Spiluttini, Vienna, Austria

Page 78 right:
Joachim Raab, Frankfurt, Germany

Case studies

Page 81:
Jork Weissmann, msp-h, Vienna, Austria

Page 82-83:
Zucchi architetti, Milan, Italy

Page 84-85:
Peter Oszvald, Bonn, Germany

Page 86-87:
Roland Halbe/artur, Stuttgart, Germany

Page 88-89:
Christian Richters, Münster, Germany

Page 90-91:
Miran Kambic, Ljubljana, Slovenia

Page 92-93:
Heinrich Helfenstein, Zurich, Switzerland

Page 95 top:
Andreas Gabriel, Munich, Germany

Page 95 bottom:
Florian Holzherr, Munich, Germany

Photographs at the start of chapters:

Page 7:
Zucchi architetti, Milan, Italy

Page 29:
Andreas Gabriel, Munich, Germany

Page 59:
Georg Aerni, Zurich, Switzerland

Page 79:
Christian Richters, Münster, Germany